Praise for *Generation Awakened*

Just as the world watched what seemed to be religious stability collapsing beneath scandals, cynicism, and skepticism, something happened among Gen-Z students on a campus in Kentucky. This volume, by one of the closest observers of the Asbury revival, shows us what happened, and why it ought to shake us, whatever our generation, out of complacency and despair. The Spirit is still on the move, and pays no attention to our forecasts and blueprints. In an era of diminished expectations, this is the book we need.

—Russell Moore, Editor in Chief, *Christianity Today*

With every outpouring of God's presence, people often line up to ask, "Where's the fruit?" In this delightful, joy-filled book, we discover the fruit of God showing up at Asbury University. By the time you finish the last page, you'll be longing for more of Jesus, His presence, His Power, and His goodness in your life. This is a gift of writing you won't want to stop reading.

—Margaret Feinberg, author of *More Power to You* and podcaster at *The Joycast*

The work of the Holy Spirit of God is always to bring glory to Jesus Christ. He is no respecter of places. A tiny college campus with one road in and out of town will do. He is not so stuffy that Facebook and Instagram can't become the primary heralds of His still small voice. A revival that started among sixteen hundred students and blazed into every shadowy corner of the world on social media seems improbable. Sarah Baldwin's account of just such an event spellbinds, ready to encourage hearts seeking to be strangely warmed.

—DT Slouffman, Director of Content, Redeeming Babel, television producer, 10-time Emmy Award winner

It is hard to believe, but this book tells a true tale. God showed up at Asbury University unexpectedly at (of all places) a chapel. God always does that—showing up unexpected in the least anticipated places. What this story shows us is that God is not done and will leave no generation without a witness. It is an honor to endorse this book. But it is all the more an honor to endorse its author—my friend Sarah Baldwin—who has faithfully stewarded what God has been doing at Asbury since everything went down. Hold on to your horses. This story is almost unbelievable.

—**A.J. Swoboda**, Ph.D., professor of Bible and Theology at Bushnell University and author of *The Gift of Thorns*

As a fellow participant, I'm grateful for Sarah's storytelling and testimony! As a fellow teammate alongside her, I was in tears remembering those sweet days and the honor to steward together. As a brother in Christ, I'm so excited for the Church and those curious about what God did for sixteen days in our midst. Pick this book up, read it, and grow in hunger for a new work in your chapels, churches, and contexts!

—**Zach Meerkreebs**, Pastor-in-Residence, Asbury University, and author

Considerable commentary on the Asbury Outpouring has originated from non-proximate voices. In *Generation Awakened* readers will get to experience Sarah's first-person account of the beauty, complexity, hunger, peace, and transformation that marked those historic 16 days in February 2023. This is a book of hope and encouragement—a detailed narration of the holy imagination and selfless hospitality that fostered a spiritual unfolding unlike anything we have seen in the 21st Century.

—**Kevin J. Brown**, PhD, President, Asbury University

How beautiful! As an eyewitness to an extraordinary work of God, Sarah has woven her own soul's encounter with God into the story of her moment-by-moment shared stewarding of an unforgettable movement of the Holy Spirit. This is a spiritually sensitive account, wrapping indescribable realities into words that invite the reader into this Outpouring of love. She describes Gen Z standing under a waterfall of holy love, drenched in the presence of Jesus. Reading her humble testimony, bathed in Scripture and lyrics of worship, some of that blessing splashed on me.

—**Linda Adams**, Bishop Emerita, Free Methodist Church

Of all the books and articles written about the 2023 Asbury Awakening/ Outpouring, *Generation Awakened* by Sarah Baldwin is unique in that it represents a vibrant, eye-witness account of the entire sixteen days from one of the central leaders inside Asbury University. This breathtaking account stirs all of the original divine moments, celebrations, emotions, and questions that we all experienced during those unforgettable days, including her reflections about how this awakening continues to stir Gen. Z, and a church in desperate need of awakening, in profound ways.

—Timothy C. Tennent, President, Asbury Theological Seminary

Generation Awakened is a riveting account of the ways God's Spirit moved at Asbury University in February 2023. Baldwin's clear prose and excellent pacing give readers a front-row seat to the Spirit's work. She tells a story of humility, struggle, grace, and transformation that will encourage and challenge anyone who wonders whether God still shows up with loving power among us.

—Amy Julia Becker, author of *To Be Made Well: An Invitation to Wholeness, Healing, and Hope*

For sixteen days in the winter of 2023, Jesus Christ visited the campus of Asbury University in an extraordinary way. Sarah Baldwin's eyewitness account is the one we have been waiting for—not because of the exceptional way Sarah humbly and skillfully stewarded the work of God on campus for those sixteen days—but because of the way she shepherded the work of God on that campus for the 3,195 days that came before and every day since. Sarah's telling of the story radiates with revealed wisdom both practical and transcendent. She will encourage your soul while equipping your hands and heart to pursue the emerging generations of young adults with the love of Jesus himself.

—J.D. Walt, Founder and Sower in Chief, Seedbed, Inc.

GENERATION
AWAKENED

GENERATION AWAKENED

An Eyewitness Account of the Powerful
Outpouring of God at Asbury

Sarah Thomas Baldwin

invite
PRESS
Plano, Texas

To Asbury University Students:
The Surrendered Class of 2023
The Courageous Class of 2024
The Ignited Class of 2025
The Restored Class of 2026
May the outpouring of God's love upon you never cease.

And to Madi, Kai, and Emily.
God's timing is perfect.

Contents

A Sacred Spark

On February 8, 2023, a few students lingered after a regular Asbury University chapel service, and the Holy Spirit sparked a flame that flared into a blaze seen around the world. Wikipedia classified it as a "phenomenon."[1] The world stopped to take note of what began as college students hungering for more of God. Over the next sixteen days, through Facebook, Instagram, TikTok, and YouTube videos, millions of shares and views grabbed media attention from all corners of the globe. What started as college students experiencing a fresh move of the Holy Spirit on Asbury's campus spontaneously combusted into a move of God upon the world.

The bonfire of God's love burned on Asbury's campus for Generation Z, and the rest of us lit the wick of our hearts to the flame of the Spirit. While critics attempt to call into question the revival's authenticity and true spontaneity, for those present during these days, these claims sound like the "wisdom of the world," foolish in God's sight (see 1 Corinthians 1:20), for we know that we could never have lit the match of the Spirit ourselves. God's love blazed tall and bright, released to the world on February 23, 2023, and it still burns to this day, as many continue to light their candles to God's flame. At least fifty thousand people arrived from over three hundred colleges and universities, more than thirty states and at least thirteen countries, to experience the lavish love of God in Wilmore, Kentucky, between

---

1. See Wikipedia, s.v. "2023 Asbury revival," accessed December 18, 2023, https://en.wikipedia.org/wiki/2023_Asbury_revival.

February 8 and February 24, 2023. But those fifty thousand only represent a portion of the multitudes touched by this extravagant expression of God's love. Whether across the internet or shared in person, the testimonies of what God did in February 2023 sparks a fresh flame of God wherever it is heard.

Much ink, multiple social media posts, and considerable conversation already note the declining church attendance in America, the growing number of people who mark "None" under "Religion" on surveys, and the loss of trust in institutions like the church and higher education. Many of us bemoan Generation Z—the generation immersed at birth or in preschool with smartphone culture—and their anxiety-laden and customized lives. While Gen X and older millennials may have appeared to be socially compelled to "make the world a better place" in their youth, it sometimes looks as though Generation Z only cares about becoming famous as an "influencer" on social media.

But what a world we are handing over! As the church, we offer Gen Z a world in which entertainment and dopamine hits from "likes" attempt to nourish souls, in which the polarization of churches over politics and racial trauma dresses up like discipleship. We leave Generation Z to be spiritually formed more by social media influencers and Netflix than by mature Christians. Instead of giving young people the saints of God, we give them celebrities. And instead of living lives of surrender to Jesus and death to self, we give them reality TV. We build walls instead of tables. Instead of being known by our love, we are known by our fear. We seek to grow faith out of the soil of security and political ideology instead of being rooted in humility and unity at the foot of the cross.

On an ordinary day in February, God showed up and awakened Generation Z with an outpouring of love that co-opted the communication methods of the day. As a torrent of God's love poured out on young adults at the foot of the cross in Hughes Auditorium at

Asbury and rippled outward around the world, we found a generation hungry and thirsty for the real Christian life of confession, repentance, and surrender. Generation Z stayed under the outpouring of God's love and experienced an overwhelming sense of the presence of Jesus, love for one another, and desire to know God. University students led us to the table of God's love. With the table set, the feast prepared, I pulled up my chair to the glorious goodness of God along with the thousands upon thousands. Gen Z's response to Jesus may be a corrective to the church that has tended to swing from either casual recreational "faith" on one side to weaponized political "faith" on the other side.

This outpouring of God's love revealed a spiritual hunger, expressed by a radical humility to steward the movement of God without taking it over, simple worship, embodied spiritual experience, and invitation to salvation and surrender. We learned revival runs on the track of relationships built with trust over time. We experienced the power of God released in multiethnic worship teams. God called forth the saints of the generations, from their twenties and thirties to their eighties and nineties, to scaffold this great move of God. Together, we experienced a fresh vision of the church.

As I share my story of the outpouring of God's love on our campus, I imagine a huge feast of the most delicious and diverse foods from around the world. My story is only one dish at the extravagant potluck of stories and experiences. The words of John 21:25 spring to life for me: "Jesus did many other things as well. If every one of them were written down, I suppose that even the whole world would not have room for the books that would be written" (NIV). While certainly not trying to compare the Asbury revival to the gospel, I resonate with the gospel writer's emotion—the good news of the 2023 movement of God and the revival it ignited could not be humanly collected and captured in their entirety.

As the vice president of student life at Asbury University, I lead the team of student affairs professionals. With many years of responsibility for the chapel program and spiritual formation at Asbury and previously at George Fox University, I am passionate for young adults to be transformed in relationship with Jesus and through mentoring and discipleship. During the spontaneous movement of God on our campus, I lived the unique role of co-convening and facilitating the core ministry team for the revival, leading in the rapidly scaling logistical management, and serving on the president's cabinet, making institutional decisions we never imagined we would make. I have sought to write a faithful telling of the days of the revival from my perspective. As you read, may the same Jesus who poured out love in Hughes Auditorium, across Wilmore, and throughout the world in those days, pour love out upon you. God's outpouring of love is for you too! *Don't miss the moment.*

Day One

February 8
Hughes Auditorium
Asbury University

Jesus answered, "Very truly I tell you, no one can enter the kingdom of God unless they are born of water and the Spirit. Flesh gives birth to flesh, but the Spirit gives birth to spirit. You should not be surprised at my saying, 'You must be born again.' The wind blows wherever it pleases. You hear its sound, but you cannot tell where it comes from or where it is going. So it is with everyone born of the Spirit."

—John 3:5–8 niv

As the Spirit was moving over the waters
Spirit, come move over us.

— "Rest on Us," Maverick City Music

Early afternoon, February 8, 2023

We are still worshipping!
—12:08 p.m.

I swipe my phone open and read the text. After dropping off my lunch tray in the dining hall, I gather up my coat and bag, click on my calendar, and note I have just enough time to stop by and see what is going on. I quickly pass the student center, closed for renovations, pass through the series of brick arches framing the walkway, and step into the back doors of the building and through the lobby, mentally reviewing what I need to get done yet that day.

I pause in the doorway of Hughes Auditorium. The voices of the Asbury Gospel Choir greet me, and the stained-glass windows shine with the afternoon sun, throwing gentle light on students caught up in praise of the faithfulness and goodness of God. Chapel officially ended a couple of hours earlier, but about thirty students remain in worship. Some stand with hands uplifted; others kneel; a few sway to the music, arms around each other, while still others sit down, backpacks stowed under their chairs, eyes shining with tears. The worship band sits along the edge of the stage, singing about the goodness of God, their faces illuminated. I breathe it all in, sensing first the presence of Jesus and then a soft soul tug to stay and worship.

It is shortly after 1:00 p.m. on February 8, 2023. Every year a few chapel services continue past their 10:50 a.m. benediction. Students love to worship, and sometimes when the worship band continues to play and the Spirit of God feels particularly close, students stay to sing. I unfold a wooden chair in one of the front rows, my work bag at my feet, ignoring the buzz of my phone in my pocket. Settling into my seat, I give myself over to the peace of the moment.

Students trickle in from each entrance of Hughes. Quietly, as if pulled by an invisible hand, students drift toward the altar or join classmates in a row of seats. A few find spots alone in a row and sit or stand, drawn into the radiant worship. The breath of God exhales upon us, and it feels like the warmth of a fire snapping in the fireplace of a chilly room—you cannot help but stand beside it.

The gentle embrace of God folds in on me. Although I have a meeting in just a few minutes, I feel my shoulders release, my breathing slow.

"Your goodness is running after, is running after me. With my life laid down, I surrender now," the students sing, and my voice joins in.[1]

I wonder whether I have to leave for an administrative meeting or if I can stay here with the students. My mind runs through the list of things that I need to follow up on. I feel the pressure of the tasks on my mental checklist, but I also feel the gentle invitation of the Holy Spirit to linger. On a small campus like ours, where staff members hold multiple roles, there is always seemingly more to do than can be humanly done. I lead the student life team, which provides support and resources for the student experience outside the classroom. With about a thousand residential students and a small team, so much rests on our shoulders. A few more minutes . . . I feel the calm like a quilt wrap around me, enclosing me in love. My eyes close, and my mind stills. The soft singing invites my soul and my heart, my spirit wanting to enter more deeply into the moment along with the students. I realize how tired I am.

My jaw unclenches and my daily tension headache starts slipping away. The voices and music hold the moment, holy and gentle, opening my spirit to another step into the presence of God. I look over at one of our team members, Liz Louden. Liz stands by the stained-glass window, a spectrum of gold, her palms turned up and her face tilted toward heaven. Madeline, the university chapel coordinator, leans into the worship in the middle of the students at the altar, her face shining. The beauty of the moment sears into my mind and my heart. God is so good to us. Our students drew us into worship, right into the heart of God.

Come rest on us.

1. Ed Cash et al., "Goodness of God," track 2 on Victory, Bethel Music, 2018, live album.

It is still early in the semester, but our whole community feels the exhaustion of the grind of the academic calendar. Students drag themselves to class on the bleak February mornings, and faculty disappear into their offices, weighed down with class preparation. I too am worn out, brittle, and stretched too thin. Tears prick at the inside of my eyelids. My soul feels like my youngest daughter's Play-Doh after being left on the counter—hardened and dried out. While I serve as a college administrator, my vocational call as a pastor energizes me to do the work of creating a community for students. But I am buried under the endless lists of student issues, campus crises, my own kids' school runs, emails, medical appointments, and administration. My life seems like a series of obligations, not like the joy of my calling. Even in this holy moment, the sense of God's presence begins to shift into a background melody as the tasks flood back into my brain.

Ping! My phone jumps in my pocket. Back to the real time of meetings and the calendar. I hesitate. Could this breath of God be meant for me too? Could I put everything on hold, like these students, and just rest in the presence of God? I close my eyes for another moment, wondering, savoring the space of the beautiful worship.

I like to say I never get tired of college students, and really, it is true. Most college students live in a liminal space between the reality of the responsibilities of adulthood and the relative simplicity of childhood. It is no accident that God often called people in the Bible during these formative years of emerging adulthood. Mary's yes to God as an emerging adult brought Jesus into the world. While David cared for sheep as a teenager, Samuel anointed him as king. Joseph started the journey that eventually saved his family from starvation when he was thrown into Pharoah's prison as a young man and began to listen to God. When she found herself in life-threatening circumstances, young Esther advocated for and championed the people of

God and saved a generation. Shadrach, Meshach, and Abednego's devotion to the ways of God almost got them burned alive, until angels intervened, and their lives became a prophetic witness even though they were "young men" (see Daniel 1:3–6). God has a habit of using young people.

College students may be more ready to respond to God than the rest of us. With hearts open to authentic relationship and willingness to receive from the Holy Spirit, young people are often God's vessels. The emerging space of becoming allows for God to move profoundly in their lives. I experience the gifts and graces of God through students. While I have been their pastor, administrator, or mentor, it is my heart that is changed and moved through walking with them. My own spiritual formation is shaped by shepherding college students through grace, freedom, and earnest discipleship.

Ping! Another text. I jolt back to the reality of what is pressing on me. My peaceful awareness of God's presence splinters into fragments.

I grab my work bag and head for the door. What sweet space! I am happy for our students. But I have a lot of things that must get done before the end of the day.

Early February 2023

February is a bleak month on campus. The word *trudge* sums up our campus in February. We trudge across campus, students, and faculty alike. The overcast sky infects most people's spirits with a gray malaise. Between the stretch of wintry days without much sun and no break from classes, February shows up as a slog to get through every year, it seemed, but especially now.

I often cross campus to my office, noting the students' heads down toward their phones or their feet, dragging themselves to class.

With their eyes drawn away from others, more likely to smile at a phone than another human, it seems that even on our small campus there are invisible barriers.

At times I feel like our students, too busy to look up, head down, shoulders tense, trying to manage things. Hurriedly sending email and texts on the go, stuck in problem-solving mode, trying to manage the complexity of student issues, I miss others' faces too, my own eyes on my phone and my brain preoccupied with competing priorities.

The last few years had worn on all of us. In the storm of the tensions of the national landscape and the divide of evangelicals over social and political issues, our small campus felt the winds of cultural struggle. When we were separated from each other by masks, quarantine and isolation, and a cloak of suspicion about each other's politics when it came to COVID restrictions, our relationships had been strained.

The Surrendered Class, the graduating class of 2023, had been with us through COVID, and in some ways I felt we had never recovered fully the loss of community from that season. But most of campus felt the pressure of national division and international insecurity and how it had made its way right into our classrooms, residence halls, and cafeteria. On top of that, February is the most grueling month on a college campus.

"February is really hard on students' mental health," one of the campus therapists reminded us. "If there are any activities you can plan in February to get them out of their dorm rooms and interacting, it's a good idea. You can expect that almost every student is feeling anxious."

College-student mental health is in crisis. Asbury surveys our students annually about their mental health, and we know that our campus reflected the national trend. Most students report feeling lonely and isolated. Anxiety continues to skyrocket across the last decade. Suicidal ideation and self-harm are reported at about 10 percent of those students seeking therapy on our campus, and we recognize that the number most likely is a low number.

Nationally, researchers describe almost half of college students reporting symptoms of depression,[2] about 9 percent report attempting suicide in the past year, and nearly 20 percent injure themselves and/or have thought about suicide.[3] Students who demonstrate these dangerous signs get help right away on our campus. But many more students who have mild anxiety or depression or experienced feelings of being overwhelmed with college life signed up for support groups and counseling or coped in other, less healthy ways, like binge-watching shows or nurturing sexual addictions.

Young adult depression and anxiety have risen steadily since the emergence of the smartphone. College professionals see students less prepared for social environments in these past years. In addition, students bring prior traumatic experiences with them to college as well as diagnosed mental health disorders. The ramifications of COVID in their middle school and high school years amplify the feelings of isolation and loss that students already carried.

Our student life team trains and prepares to manage increasingly complex student mental health issues. We are familiar with the insides of ERs and even psychiatric units for students who were in crisis. Along with mental health concerns, we watch our students become increasingly polarized around social issues, such as vaccines, masks, and politics. Where once our students engaged in debate and conversation about political issues around cafeteria tables, the conversations now move to Twitter and grow increasingly absent publicly. Relationships fracture. Politics creates too many divides and

2.   Preeti Vankar, "Percentage of College Students with Symptoms of Depression in the United States in 2022-2023," Statista, November 29, 2023, https://www.statista.com/statistics/1126279/percentage-of-college-students-with-depression-us/.

3.   Steven Reinberg, "One in Five College Students So Stressed They Consider Suicide," Association of American Universities, September 10, 2018, https://www.aau.edu/research-scholarship/featured-research-topics/one-five-college-students-reported-thoughts-suicide.

discomfort. As the nation grapples with racial tensions, grief, and lament at injustice, our own students of color share more with the primarily white administrators and faculty about their feelings of loss and lack of safety in the world. I held the grief and tension of the students with my colleagues. The priority list of student needs grew longer and the budgets tighter in small universities like ours.

We feel the tension.

Our students also represent a range of Christian experiences. Some of them arrive on campus with little practical contact with church or Christian practices. Others have mature faith with Christians parents and committed youth pastors who discipled them. Students do not need to be professing Christians to come to Asbury. The founder of Asbury University, John Wesley Hughes, had a vision to prepare young men and women to be saved, fully committed to God, and prepared for service. From the beginning, Asbury's evangelistic heart fueled academic rigor. At the core of Asbury University is dedication to academic excellence and spiritual vitality. The heartbeat of Asbury is to shape and send earnest disciples of Jesus into the world as leaders in every sector of society. With the dramatic challenges in culture and shifting dynamics of the influence of the church in the world, the need for discipleship, mental health support, and pastoral care to accomplish this mission has only steepened.

Belong, Become, Be Set Apart. These guiding words shape the campus community. The pulse of Asbury is for students to belong to Jesus and in real friendship with one another. The hope is for students to become, by belonging to God and one another, more like Jesus and who they were created to be, in order to be set apart for the work of God they are called to do.

As a student life team, we know our students are facing spiritual and emotional battles. While they go through the motions of showing up at chapel and attending class, most of them hold daily pain, stress, and doubt. Social media influencers disciple this generation more than pastors and mentors do. As a team, we share in discouragement over the anxiety with which our students live and how little of the hope, freedom, and goodness of Jesus they experience.

Even as I go to meeting after meeting to administrate and shape campus culture, what we need more than ever was the deep love of Jesus to immerse us as a campus community.

I also need the deep love of Jesus to immerse me.

3:30 p.m., February 8, 2023

I meet our president, Kevin Brown, on the front steps of Hughes as we jog up the stairs. Hughes Auditorium is an iconic brick building with several sets of steps leading to a pillared entrance. A semicircle forms the entrance of Asbury University with the campus's oldest buildings: Hughes, Morrison Hall, the Hager Administration Building, and Glide-Crawford Women's Residence Hall. With early 1900s formality, the buildings create the front perimeter of the campus. Through a grove of trees and across the street is Asbury Theological Seminary. Born from Asbury University in 1923, it shares a rich heritage of Wesleyan theology and the holiness tradition.

I attend a meeting about priorities for student food service for a couple of hours, and I see another meeting scheduled with Kevin in the president's office. But instead of meeting in his office, we meet on the steps of Hughes without any conversation. We just know we have to be in Hughes. Slipping into the chapel, I note a few faculty and staff are gathered around the back. Earlier, Kevin had sent an email to the whole community, inviting them to come and experience this sweet move of God among our students. In the two hours since I left, more have gathered. Now about 150 students and a few rows of faculty and staff are present.

The worship team continues singing, standing around the piano. "Come rest on us," they sing earnestly. I recognize most of the worship team is still the Asbury Gospel Choir. The Gospel Choir is a student ensemble led by a staff member, Ben Black, who is also an admissions counselor. As a multiethnic team, the Asbury Gospel Choir led worship this morning in chapel, and a Wilmore resident and spouse of a seminary student, Georges Dumain, joined them. I do not know Georges, but his whole body seems to be a conduit of the Spirit. From his smile to his voice in worship, praise pours out of him. Ben's hands dance across the piano, and Georges leans over his shoulder. The singing closes the distance between heaven and earth, and the beauty of the voices capture me. Student Gospel Choir members move side to side and sway to the music, hands open to heaven. After five hours, with no sign of stopping, the Gospel Choir still pours forth the good news in song. The joy on the platform radiates out into Hughes like sunbeams throughout the partially filled 1500-seat auditorium.

Ben's wife, Madeline Black, is our university chapel coordinator and we work closely together planning worship services. Madeline is there as well, her face wet with tears and real joy across her features. As a recent Asbury University graduate and a current Asbury Seminary student, I know from experience Madeline lives out her theology of worship with an obvious love of Jesus. Although Madeline is only in her early twenties, I deeply appreciate the wisdom and discernment she brings to our chapel program. Madeline believes worship is the center of the Christian's experience, always pressing for each service to be reflective of worshipping Jesus. I walk up the aisle and join her. Madeline and I are a tight team. As the vice president of student life, I oversee the chapel program and Madeline supports me. We work alongside the university pastor, Greg Haseloff, to hold the formation and worship of the chapel experience. Planning three worship services a week for a congregation of a thousand is not an easy endeavor. Madeline and I lean into this work to "serve the chapel," as we say.

"This is amazing," I whisper. "I can't believe it."

"I know, I know. God is so good," Madeline replies and leans into a hug.

I linger in a stunned and happy silence. I cannot put words onto the presence of God in the space. Madeline and I prayed and prepared for chapel with Greg in great hope and love for our students that the preaching and singing would help them experience the powerful presence of the Holy Spirit. To see it happening . . . well . . . words cannot describe the experience.

More students come to the altar, foreheads pressing on the rail, shoulders shaking in quiet tears. Students now cover the middle section of the chapel. Some raise hands, others stand with palms up, and still others simply stand silently, taking it all in like me. Bibles and notebooks are open as a few journal. Small clusters of students pray together. The Spirit of God in the space hovers with invitation and everyone seems to feel it.

Along the back and at the sides, some of our faculty and staff exchange teary-eyed looks and each finds his or her way to a seat. A full row of twenty team members from the admissions office are present. A few of us stand in a circle at the side, with words of both incredulity and belief. God is moving. God is moving! How can it be? How can it not be? "Spirit, come move over us," a voice sings out. The Spirit is indeed moving across this space.

This is remarkable, I wonder. *This is different.* Although students linger after chapel on occasion, this is different. Students just keep coming and now faculty and staff join as well.

I walk back up the aisle toward the front entrance, which is at the back of the auditorium away from the stage. Sitting down on a padded folding chair against the wall, I join two women staff friends who are praying fervently. Tears run down their faces and into their laps. One of the women takes my hand and says, "Please pray with us. We are praying for our kids. We want them to experience this kind of movement of the Spirit." I join in prayer, and we pray for our kids, our husbands, and these beautiful students. We feel the press of the love of God in the room and in our own hearts for our students. We pray that what is moving and stirring will seal the love of God on each person present.

As I lift my damp eyes, I see a few students come in the back, phones in their hands, with backpacks and winter jackets. Their eyes meet mine, and we exchange looks of awe.

"I had to get here as fast as I could!"

One student flies through the doors, almost panting from running up the steps.

"My phone is going crazy," says another student.

"People are knocking on the classroom doors and saying you've got to come!" claims another.

"My classes are canceled this afternoon. Everyone just wants to be here in Hughes."

"Everyone is texting you have to be here," explains the last student, adjusting her backpack and slipping her iPhone into a side pocket.

The students stop before going down the aisle and take in the sight before them with obvious awe. Their friends and classmates appear lost in prayer and worship. I wipe away a tear in the corner of my eye. We all feel the wonder together—students, faculty, and administrators.

6:30 p.m.

Grilled cheese sandwiches, baby carrots with ranch dressing, and chicken nuggets are on the menu for dinner. My husband, Clint, and I sit with our two younger kids for dinner. Kai, age ten, is in fourth grade, and Emily, age six is in preschool. Madi, our oldest, is away at graduate school in Ireland.

"We are parenting across the life span," I quip when people ponder the age differential. Truth is, over a decade of infertility is reflected between our graduate school daughter, Madi, and our son, Kai. It is a story of God's goodness and waiting all of its own. Emily inhabits a story of God's goodness as well with an extra chromosome identifying her with Down syndrome. Emily's life is a gift and grace to us, although I did not know that to be true at the beginning.

I finish the school run, picking up both kids who had stayed late at their after-school programs, and make a fast dinner, listening to the usual about school, soccer, and homework. To our family gathered around the table, it seems a normal Wednesday. Clint had stopped by that afternoon to see for himself what was happening in Hughes, but now the focus is on our kids; our family time around the table is one of the best parts of the day. The first moments of the day, dinnertime, bedtime, these are the active prayers that make up our days.

My eye catches the quote Madi painted for me as a Christmas present. My life is full to overflowing, and each breath is a prayer:

How I live is pray.
How I pray is breathe.

I read a book once about how parents "pray the hours." The psalmist talks about praising the Lord seven times a day for his righteous ways (Psalm 119:164). The early church members in Acts prayed throughout the day, notably at 3:00 p.m. and midnight. Way back in the sixth century, Saint Benedict named prayer for each hour of the day for monastics and those who followed a devout religious life. The day begins with lauds, or morning prayer. Terce follows at around 9:00 a.m.; then sext (noon); none (around 3:00 p.m.); vespers, or evensong; and finally, compline, or night prayer. You can also do a matins, or vigils, prayer ranging from 2 a.m. to dawn.

Parents pray these hours with the practice of our presence. Our rhythms of active prayer connect with waking children in the morning, midday and afternoon snacks, dinner, baths, stories, and tuck-ins. (And more than we would prefer, middle-of-the-night wakings.) As we walk through the hours of the day in the rhythm of children, we "pray the hours" as we go. Taking note of the clock and time as it passes, we do the work of caregiving, of being present. This is holy work. As caregivers of others, we are present to others' needs and the routines and limits of family life. As we actively pray the hours with our breath and bodies, as we do the emotional, spiritual, and physical work of parenting, we know that these hours are holy.

In this way, gathering around a table, evening walks, and stories form the prayer of the hours for our children. These gentle rhythms teach them the predictability of the love of God through the lives and hearts of their parents.

I love to be present for these rhythms. As a mom who has worked outside the home for the entirety of the twenty-three years I have been a mother, I found that these gentle rhythms anchor our family life. I have a job that stretches across a lot of responsibilities and commitments. I learned that two nights a week is about all I can regularly sustain being away from my family. Although I certainly must be away more occasionally, two nights a week is my rule of life. Our campus community is used to me bringing my children to evening events and cafeteria meals. It is a way of life to be immersed in a college environment. I actively pray the hours as we share life with the campus and live out the way of being a family anchored to one another.

As we clear the table, my husband reminds me he has a video call for his work that evening starting at 7:00p.m. I want to go back—I need to go back—to Hughes that evening. I will take the children with me. I don't want to be away from them this evening. I want them to experience the profound love of Jesus that our students are experiencing.

Our house is at the edge of campus. With kids hand in hand, we walk to Hughes. I try to explain what is happening, how God is stirring the waters at Asbury and that I don't know how long it will last. I share how I want them to experience it, to taste and see the goodness of God.

We enter through the campus green side of Hughes and slip in the side doors, and I take a moment to get my bearings. Since I left, several hundred more people have arrived, mostly college students. But I also see the faces of faculty and staff and a few from our surrounding Wilmore community. I wonder how they heard. A good part of the floor of Hughes is full with maybe five hundred people.

Worship continues with the Asbury Gospel Choir. The same band. I make a mental note of how long they have led. At least eight hours. I wonder if they stopped for dinner. The altar remains full and growing, with two or three students deep, bending over in prayer, hearts pouring out in worship and earnest prayer. I look for Madeline and she is still there, sharing the piano bench with Ben. I see the chapel speaker of the day, Zach Meerkreebs, Greg, and a few other faculty members and student life team members praying with students. I find a front row seat for me and the Baldwin team "juniors," as Clint and I call them. Kai leans back in a chair, and Emily finds a place on the floor with a paint-by-water book and brush.

I breathe it all in. I look up at the seats in the balcony that are mostly empty, where freshmen students sit during the chapel hour. The middle section, where sophomores sit, is mostly full, and half of the junior and senior sections that flank it are full. For me, the wooden interior of Hughes glows with the singing and memories of the students who had come before. I had been one of those students. I had sat in these seats as a twenty-year-old and listened to my classmates belt out class hymns, listened to energetic preachers proclaiming the good news. In many ways, my spiritual identity was forged in these seats. I prayed at the altar, journaled chapel notes, listened intently, and surely also daydreamed when listening to less exciting preaching. Thirty years ago, as I began my adult life, some of my profound spiritual commitments happened here.

There is something about this place. One of our alumni and professors Chris Bounds preached a sermon in which he said, "God is everywhere all the time, but not everywhere in the same way." I keep coming back to this thought. The presence of God is sweet and close in Hughes. While no one has to come to Hughes to experience God, I cannot deny that many people encounter Jesus there at the altar. I too remember surrendering my life at the altar and doing hard spiritual and emotional work on my knees. God's presence fills Hughes in a unique way.

A lot of life had happened both hard and beautiful in the years since I was a student. My faith was stretched and questioned, even doubted. It waned, then strengthened. With the challenge of the recent years, weariness permeated my being. I also missed the intensity of my faith in days before there was so much of life to hold. I felt overwhelmed with creating space for everyone else, students and my children alike.

Each class has a class hymn and a class name. As a member of the Servant Class, the words of my class hymn wove their way into my heart:

> Take my life and let it be
> consecrated, Lord, to thee.
> Take my moments and my days;
> let them flow in endless praise,
> let them flow in endless praise.[4]

---

4.   Frances R. Havergal (1836–1879), "Take My Life and Let It Be."

I realize this is what I am experiencing now, these students are in an endless circle of worship and praise. It warms my heart and my being. My son, Kai, leans his head over toward me, and we simply rest in God's Spirit. The Spirit of God moves with goodness, kindness, and invitation.

Jesus, I pray simply, again and again*, take my life and let it be. Meet these students in their place of deepest need.*

It is hard to stay seated because so many people stop by to share a word of excitement or wonder at what God is doing. And more students are on their way!

"Sarah, I am hearing that University of Kentucky's student worship finished early and is on their way down."

"I just heard that students from Indiana Wesleyan are on their way."

"I just got a text that a group from Eastern Kentucky University are coming."

"Ohio Christian is sending students!"

I am dumbstruck. "How do they even know what is happening?"

"I guess students posted on Instagram and TikTok. They're also texting their friends."

Amazing. More students are coming! My heart leaps! God is doing something incredibly special here.

Spontaneously, students share testimonies at the microphone. Sitting on the edge of stage, they each share a word about what they are experiencing. A group of students make a prayer line down the aisle from shoulder to shoulder to put their hands on a student who is sharing what God is doing.

Zach encourages the students to stand and repent openly. As each person repents, others join them in confession. The students gather and lay hands on one another, repenting, confessing, proclaiming healing and freedom over one another.

In his early thirties, with a beard and tattoos, Zach has an unassuming presence and easy-to-connect-with style that makes him approachable to students. Zach preached in chapel that morning about God's deep love for us—a love that gets our attention like an itchy sweater. Zach's message stirred students' hearts in the Spirit as he preached the theme of the love of God:

> Until I am experiencing the love of Jesus—until you experience the love of God—you will not be able to love in the way you want to . . . We love God because he first loved us. Some of us need to sit in the love of God. To taste and see in the power of the Holy Spirit. If you want to become love in action, you start by prostrating yourself in the love of God. You have to experience the love of God to be the love of God. I pray that this word sits on you like an itchy sweater. You got an itch, you just have to take care of it. So, experience the love of God!

Zach prayed for our students, for the Holy Spirit to pour out love upon them: "Jesus, do a new thing in our midst. Revive us by Your love."

May the love of God be so itchy you can't stop thinking about it; you have to deal with it. The whole campus seemed to be an experiencing a contagious outbreak of God's love.

Students love Zach for his vulnerability about his own story, filled with trauma and loss and his zeal for the Lord. Over the past couple of years, Zach had served as a chapel and retreat speaker, as well as an assistant volunteer soccer coach.

Greg leans over a group of athletes in prayer. Greg's sensitive face and kind eyes pour forth the love of Jesus on the students in a daily manner. But on this day, the athletes come with their teams, hearts stirring for this kind of radical Jesus experience. No one loves our students more than Greg. With a heart of compassion and kindness, Greg shepherds them, seeking them out and knowing their names. He seems to know every student and personifies the love of Jesus upon them.

As I my eyes meet Zach's, we share a look of awe and wonder. We could never imagine this!

"Spread the word to our team we need to meet somewhere and talk," I encourage. "Let's go downstairs under Hughes."

With Emily on my hip, Zach, me and a group of administrators and friends of Asbury assemble in the hallway under Hughes.

Along the hallways of the basement of Hughes are the composites of the graduates gone before, the faces of the thousands that sat in Hughes' seats, knelt at the altar, and experienced God. We celebrated the fiftieth anniversary of the 1970 revival just a couple of years before, and we walked by these faces of the 1970 graduating class as we went to our meeting spot. We knew that God showed up in Hughes Auditorium in unique ways. We shared a family story of how the Spirit of God fell on people in Hughes in an unusual way.

The 1970 revival wove many threads into my own call to ministry and spiritual life story. Almost everyone who played a key spiritual role in my discipleship as a teenager and college student experienced transformation in Hughes in 1970 through the power of God. Whether I know it or not in that moment, the story unfolding in me as I stand in the circle started in the years before through the move of the Holy Spirit.

The circle waits in an amazed silence for a few moments. Strains of music float down from above, and the sound of footsteps and chairs opening and closing reach our ears, as our eyes catch the faces of the students who experienced revival in years past on the walls.

One of the people present in our circle, David Thomas, leans into the center, his voice serious and earnest. "I think you may have something here," he says quietly. We all look at each other, various levels of wonder and surprise on our faces. What is happening?

2

The First Yes

February 2023
Asbury University
Hughes Auditorium

"For nothing will be impossible with God." Then Mary said, "Here am I, the servant of the Lord; let it be with me according to your word." Then the angel departed from her.

—*Luke 1:37–38*

Way maker, miracle worker . . .
My God, this is who You are.

—*Sinach, "Way Maker"*

I think you may have something here." David Thomas' words echo in our circle. As a theologian of spiritual awakenings and a scholar of revival history, David encourages us to open our minds and hearts to what may be happening in our midst. Throughout the next days, David's exhortation becomes instrumental in heightening awareness of the movement of God upon us. While David may have arrived to support Zach and see with his own eyes God moving in Hughes, David himself becomes grafted into the ministry and leadership of the movement almost immediately.

We wait silently for a moment, our hearts stirring, the growing sense of God's presence drawing us together with a common heart for our students to experience spiritual awakening.

We know God worked in powerful ways in Hughes over the decades. The stories of the 1970 revival spring to my mind. My memory fills with the voices of mentors who shared with me their experiences: "An irresistible pull." "I had to hold on to the radiator in the back to keep me from going forward." "We prayed for a year at 8:00 a.m. for God to bring revival to Asbury."

The winter quarter at Asbury in 1970 opened with a restless and dissenting student body according to several editorials in the January 28 *Asbury Collegian*.[1] Apparently, frustrated over rules and fractured by what some called a rebellious spirit, the student body was restless. The students must have also been affected by the social and political upheaval of the culture. It was in that context that God showed up. Distinguished evangelist, author, and professor Robert Coleman writes about the 1970 revival: "In a way awesome to behold, God had taken over the campus. Caught up in the wonder of it, a thousand students remained for days in the college auditorium—not to demand more freedom or to protest the Establishment, but to confess their sin and to sing the praises of their Saviour."[2]

Revival fell before I was born and influences me to this day.

But it was not just revival in 1970. The waters had stirred in Hughes across the century. February 1905, February 1921, February 1950, March 1958, February 1970, March 1992, February 2006. The presence of God falls in this sacred space. Many calls to ministry and salvation around the nation are traced to these moves of God.

Now, in 2023, fifty-three years after the 1970 revival, which brought waves of renewal of faith, we again feel divided and isolated from each other, in some ways as a campus, but certainly in the broader Christian context. Is God moving again?

1. Joe Thacker, Jr., *Asbury College: Vision and Miracle* (Nappanee, IN: Evangel, 1990), 222.
2. Robert E. Coleman, ed., *One Divine Moment* (Old Tappan, NJ: Spire, 1970), 13–14.

Jeannine Brabon, an alumna and person of bold prayer, discipled me as a twelve- and thirteen-year-old. Jeannine spent her life as a missionary in Colombia in some of the darkest places in the world—in a Colombian prison and in ministry to members of the drug cartel. I remember sitting at the table with her, during her furlough, in the One Mission Society Student Center just off the campus where she lived. She told me the stories of how a small group of students prayed on class days at 8:00 a.m. for God to move for a year before the 1970 revival ignited. I know a small group of students now pray regularly for revival at the World Gospel Ministry center just a quarter mile from campus. Is it time now for God to move for our students like before?

Those of us in the circle know our Asbury story of how God had moved at Hughes. We do not want to stop or limit what God is doing. *Yes*, we will keep Hughes open overnight so if God continues to move and our students respond, the space will be open.

I am concerned about the college students coming from other places. If we close Hughes at midnight, where will they go? It makes sense to leave it open and then reconvene in the morning to discern the movement of the Spirit at that point.

I feel a little hesitant at the same time. In my administrative role, I feel responsibility for the safety of our students. Leaving Hughes open overnight, with students arriving at all hours from other campuses, seems a bit risky. Nevertheless, God is on the move. I do not want to get in the way. We pray for safety, and I reach out to campus safety for extra presence in and around Hughes.

We said *YES*. Little did we know this moment would be the first of what would become thousands upon thousands of yeses. In the moment, we felt absolute clarity that the experience expressed what we knew of the Holy Spirit—gentle, invitational, full of love and kindness, almost irresistible. We knew we could only say *YES*.

The scriptures are full of *YES*. I wonder about when Mary said, "Let it be to me according to your word." She had no idea what was to come and what was really being asked of her. She must have felt the wonder, awe, and holiness of the moment. The answer in her spirit seemed clear and true and right. That first night of revival, what was happening seemed true and right to us too.

From my perspective as I write this, I track back the story of what God did at Asbury to this simple "yes." At that moment we said: Yes, we will keep Hughes open. Yes, we will be open to seeing what God wanted to do.

Later, our cabinet will gather and reflect on the movement of God at Asbury. If God had given us twenty-four hours' notice, would we have said yes? No. If God had given us a month's notice, would have said yes? No. If God had given us a year's notice, would have said yes? No. If God had laid out the scope of what was ahead of us and asked us, "Will you climb this mountain?" Most likely, we would have discerned a no. It would be too much. Too much on our people, too many resources required, too much wear and tear on the building, too much time and energy expected from everyone. Surely, God, we must be hearing incorrectly. We would not have had the holy imagination to say yes to what God was asking even with all we knew of how God had stirred revival for the past century. In our humanity, we would have seen obstacles and strain. And so, God, in His mercy and goodness, invited us into this monumental journey one small step at a time, by simply and undeniably showing up. We could say no at any point, and God would find another way to rest upon His people. God certainly did not depend on us. Yet, the Holy Spirit invited us to partner in the redeeming and freeing work of Jesus, one step at a time. *Would we take this one step?*

I pull out my phone and text to a team of thirteen:

Dear friends, what an honor to see God move among us. We are planning on having Hughes open overnight. It would be helpful to have at least one team member present.

I follow the text with a list of times: 10:00 p.m.–midnight, midnight–2:00 a.m., 2:00 a.m.–4:00 a.m., 4:00 a.m.–6:00 a.m., and so on. I will take the 4:00 a.m. shift. Responding quickly, the team covers the other shifts within minutes.

Emily runs in circles around me, and I try to manage her and finish texting the Asbury team. I will get my kids home and to bed and then come back in the morning. As I pass through Hughes again, the number who gather is obviously growing. One of my dearest spiritual mentors and friends, Koby Miller, is on the back row, bringing her support with physical presence. She is not the only one. Another friend and lifelong Asbury team member, John Morley, texts me, "There's as many saints as students here!" Truly, the community of older-generation saints are arriving, their very presence holding Jesus.

Wilmore is a quaint, two-stoplight town on a dead-end road. The main highway that runs through Wilmore leads you into, but not across, the Kentucky River. Surrounded by horse farms, black fences, and rolling hills, Wilmore is a beautiful small town. Asbury University and Asbury Seminary frame the main thoroughfare with stately red brick buildings and two distinguished chapels. Three churches host the street corners, along with a gas station and a sub shop. A city of about six thousand more or less, with the same mayor for forty-seven years, Wilmore has not changed much in the last decades. A few parks, a handful of mom-and-pop restaurants, several artisan businesses in the small downtown, the ancient IGA grocery store, a retirement community, an elementary school, and about twenty small nonprofit ministries join the quiet activity of this Mayberry-like community.

Wilmore is home for the saints of the Church. It would be hard to find more Christians per capita than the little town of Wilmore. Retired missionaries and pastors fill its houses, along with seminary students preparing for ministerial appointments and university graduates who settled to raise families in its friendly streets. Wilmore may be the only town where the plumber has a Master of Divinity and your real estate agent is a retired pastor. If you are wondering about Wilmore, just look at its water tower. Residents joke that while Paris has the Eiffel Tower and New York City has the Statue of Liberty, Wilmore has the water tower. On top of that white water tower is perched a white lighted cross that glows across the night sky above the softball and baseball fields, announcing clearly that Wilmore belongs to God.

I have left and come back to Wilmore twice as an adult, once from Michigan and once from Oregon. As my calling to ministry and leadership unfolded, I knew I had to leave. Sometimes the proximity of Christians and Christian institutions made me feel as if I were in a greenhouse, carefully tended and watered, but my roots and branches had no place to grow. A long-term resident chided me, telling me it was good to leave Wilmore. "Too much salt makes the dead sea," she joked with a bit of truth in her eye.

Wilmore could be a layered place. Between the layers of institutions, church culture, and more PhDs than were probably necessary for any one town, there is a lot to process. My own spiritual journey navigated the underlying expectations that I bumped into of what it meant to be a good enough Christian and if it was doctrine and rules that saved you or the condition of your heart. As I wrestled with this as a young adult, I did find Wilmore mentors and friends who showed me lives marked with grace and love, not legalism. Naming the decade of my twenties as from "law to love," I grew deep and wide in the love of Jesus, ready to be transplanted into different soil following God's call.

But this time, coming to Asbury in my current role, I felt as though the Wilmore soil was just what my family and I needed. Nutrient-rich and cultivated, this small town was the place where I found peace and felt only gratitude to raise my youngest kids with its kindly neighbors and Christian worldview. Wherever you live, people have real problems, real heartbreak, and real financial and physical challenges. Wilmore was no different in that way. But the spiritual maturity of the place scaffolded the pain and hardship of life with godly support in many unique ways in between its spires and streets. One thing was certainly true about this community; the saints of God lived here, and they showed up when the Holy Spirit moved.

That night, amid a new move of God, I recognize the faces of the saints, the ones who were my seminary professors, neighbors, and friends, who gather to see what God is doing with our students. To pray with our students, to worship with them, to bask in the love of Jesus.

And a child shall lead them, my lifelong friend and team member, Michelle Kratzer, messages me. Generation Z is leading our community to the altar of Hughes.

Gen Z is saying yes to an invitation to feast in the Spirit, and we are pulling up chairs to the table and joining them.

February 9, 3:45 a.m.

My phone alarm buzzes, and my head moves off the pillow and falls back again. I didn't sleep well for the few hours I was in bed. I really don't want to miss my shift. I stumble into the kitchen; make coffee; find my Bible, notebook, and favorite pen; slide my feet into a pair of warm socks and clogs; and head across campus. As I walk, I wonder what I will find. Will Hughes be empty? Will it be over? No matter what, it was a sweet move of God for our students. I feel grateful to have been an eyewitness to it.

The side door of Hughes is the one unlocked, and I go around the back of the building to reach it. As I turn the corner of the building, I see the tall, stained-glass windows pouring out yellow-gold light from the interior into the night sky. As soon as I see the windows, I know that it is not over. God is still in Hughes!

My spirit quickens, and I slip into the building. About twenty-five students are scattered in seats around the auditorium. A couple of students are at the piano bench, singing together with little actual musicality. I grin to myself. Students are settled around the room in small clusters or alone, praying, writing, and pondering. I look up to the balcony and I notice a couple of cots set up for students to sleep. In the far corner, a student is asleep on a twin mattress he must have hauled from his dorm room. I locate the last shift team member, we connect, and she fills me in on the details. The worship team left about an hour ago. It was a quiet night. Some of the students from other schools arrived and were either here or had found a place to stay the night.

I find a seat about a quarter of the way up on the right side, facing the stage. With coffee and my Bible, I settle into my seat, taking in the moment and sealing it away in my heart. It is still happening. God is still on the move, and students are still responding. Incredible.

"God, this is amazing," I breathe.

I am reading the Bible in a year-long reading plan. I have never made it through the whole Bible in a year. But when 2023 dawned, I felt a sense that this was the year. I flip to my chapters for the day. My portion for this day is Exodus 19–21, the part where Moses goes through the wilderness with the Israelites. God calls Moses up the mountain and gives him the promise that if the Israelites obey His voice and keep his covenant, they will be a priestly kingdom and a holy nation. I bracket a few verses with my pen.

> Then the LORD said to Moses, "I am going to come to you in a dense cloud, in order that the people may hear when I speak with you and so trust you ever after." (Exodus 19:9)

A dense cloud . . . the presence of God . . . thick upon us. The presence of God felt like a cloud settled on our students.

Scripture uses the imagery of clouds to tell us the story of God:

> And as Aaron spoke to the whole congregation of the Israelites, they looked toward the wilderness, and the glory of the Lord appeared in the cloud. (Exodus 16:10)

> And when the priests came out of the holy place, a cloud filled the house of the Lord, so that the priests could not stand to minister because of the cloud; for the glory of the Lord filled the house of the Lord. (1 Kings 8:10–11)

> The LORD is king! Let the earth rejoice; let the many coastlands be glad! Clouds and thick darkness are all around him, righteousness and justice are the foundation of his throne. (Psalms 97:1–2)

> Then I looked, and there was a white cloud, and seated on the cloud was one like the Son of Man, with a golden crown on his head, and a sharp sickle in his hand! (Revelation 14:4)

I sit with this for a moment. Surely, the presence of the Lord has settled upon us like a cloud.

My eyes drift to the words inscribed near the ceiling above the stage, "Holiness unto the Lord." We are not a culture and a world that understands much about holiness these days. Even among Christians, holiness gets translated to "holier-than-thou" and an old-fashioned sanctimonious way of being. Instead of being about behavior, holiness is about the intimacy of the Spirit of God taking up residence in our whole being. Our hearts after God's heart. God's heart after our hearts. Holiness is all of God for all of us. As a chapel speaker once said, "The deal of the century! The bargain of the universe! All of You for all of me!" When the Spirit of God came and hovered over us, it was the holiness of God settling on us, creating an intimate space between us and God.

It is growing quieter now. A few more students leave. I notice our president, Kevin, and his wife, Maria, slip into one of the back rows, heads bowed in prayer. My 6:00 a.m. relief shows up. I need to get home and help the kids get ready for school. I stretch a bit, grateful for the quiet morning in the ocean of God's presence.

God showed up, and the students responded. It was holy and enough. As students go to class as normal and talk about the day before, I know I will treasure these hours. A day of work and parenting spreads out ahead of me and so I give God thanks and walk home to wake up my children.

February 9, 10:30 a.m.

The floor of Hughes is full of new students arriving. Nothing is stopping or slowing down. I text a small group:

Let's meet at 10:30 a.m.

Greg, Zach, Madeline, and I sit on the edge of the platform in prayerful conversation about how to steward the ongoing open worship. Madeline arranged for various students to play and sing at the piano. Ben and Georges are coming back at 10:50 a.m., the beginning of the "dead hour." No classes are held from 10:50 to noon, and we expect that even more students will be drawn back to worship. Classes continue, not officially called off, and students come around their class times, eager to continue to worship with their classmates.

Greg's sense is to open the space for testimonials. Zach feels as though God generously gave him a message of invitation. Both seem right.

We also wrestle with a couple of questions regarding livestream and lyrics. Madeline explains, "It's hard enough to be vulnerable just with the people of Hughes; let's leave it off." The president's cabinet agrees to keep the livestream off to create more space for our students to be authentic in what they share. We livestream chapel, but we have no precedent to livestream everything in Hughes. The world doesn't need to know what the students confess and share openly and honestly with our community.

Greg shares that a few people request lyrics that may distract from the focus on Jesus. As we sort it out together, none of us want to take away from the gentle flow of the presence of God yesterday and how we experience God move. No lyrics.

I cancel my meetings without thought. I have to be here, present to what God is doing, leaning into this divine moment with my whole being. I need this too. I need to see and breathe the presence of God.

The students' testimonies are powerful. Words of repentance, confession, and blessing overflow. Students pray over other students. A contagious sense of freedom and goodness permeates the room. More and more students arrive from campus and surrounding schools. Many do not want to leave and stay for hours in a reverent state of awe and wonder when they hear their friends repenting and turning to Jesus. Students confess sin and share pain.

"I have a porn addiction," one student throws out and falls back into his seat, exhaling deeply, then covers his face with his hands in grief.

"I feel so alone. I feel as though no one sees me," a female student gets out through tears. Students come forward like a wave, surrounding her in embrace.

"I am not a Christian. I don't even know what you all are talking about. How do I follow Jesus?" another student cries as he holds out his hands. "I just need someone to tell me."

"I need healing."

"I want more of Jesus."

"I wanted to kill myself. Jesus saved me."

"Depression and anxiety no longer have control over my life!" Greg, his eyes filled with a mix of joy and tears, stands beside one of our students, Zara,[3] as she shares her testimony. For over half of her life her identity resided in anxiety and depression. The Lord has convicted her to give up anger and resentment and release control at the foot of the cross. Zara shares that for the first time in her life, she has left all of it at the feet of Jesus and has not tried to take it back up again.

"My God is bigger than my depression! My God is bigger than my anxiety! Jesus walked out of the grave, and you can too, because I did!" As she speaks, Greg's own heart is overcome with gratitude to God. Not only has he walked with Zara pastorally, but Zara's story touches his own story. Greg lost his father and brother to suicide as a young adult. His own story and spiritual calling is shaped by the deep pain of loss. As he hears Zara's testimony of walking out of the grave of anxiety and getting up from the coffin of depression in the power of Jesus, his own being resonates with this truth like the ringing of a bell. Healing is possible; freedom is possible.

This is how it happens all day. One testimony of freedom and truth from one heart spurs joy within another heart. The students experience contagious freedom, contagious joy, contagious love.

Anxiety and depression may be the calling card of this generation, but students testify to the power of God's healing at work in their lives. Although we encourage students (and anyone) to remain on prescribed medication for depression and anxiety and to continue to work with their counselor or doctor, we also see God heal and restore lives in front of our eyes. Through the power of medicine or the power of the Spirit, or both, freedom through Jesus abounds.

Greg kneels with students in prayer at the altar, bending over them, interceding for students in the way a shepherd who knows his sheep goes after the lost one. The altar is heaped five and six rows of students deep. I lean over students as well, my heart praying, *You are the beloved of God. You belong to God. May the Lord bring you free-*

---

3. Not her real name.

dom in every way. Many Asbury staff and faculty pray with students, kneeling beside the altar on the floor in the aisles, tissue boxes beside them, listening to the students' stories and sealing the work of God over them in prayer.

A few students bring their musical instruments from their rooms and join in the worship. Cello, violin, bongos, and student voices seamlessly blend in, and the worship team grows, unrehearsed, unplanned, simply responding to the invitation of Jesus. Pure joy exudes from their faces. Tears fall. Voices lift with melody and authenticity up to Jesus.

This is a divine moment. The words of Dennis Kinlaw, president of Asbury during the 1970 revival, come to me, and I text the quote to a friend:

> Give me one divine moment when God acts, and I say that moment is far superior to all the human efforts of man through the centuries.

This is a holy and divine moment in the lives of these students.

Late in the afternoon, weariness catch up with some of us, me included. Madeline organizes worship teams for the evening with her husband, Ben. There is no sign of students leaving, but even so, I start to wonder: How long will this divine moment continue? Forty-eight hours? It seems impossible, and yet, seeing the response, possible.

We need a plan. Someone on the ministry team needs to be here all the time—or maybe two of us. It is too much for one person to steward. Many community saints, faculty, and staff wade into the sea of students to pray over them and with them. But pastoral stewardship of the space and overall ministry is needed. We feel incredible responsibility for our students and the others joining them. We plan for two of us at a time to be there for the rest of the evening.

We will regroup with a gentle structure to the worship at 7:00 p.m. Zach texts us a prayer.

Jesus. Thank you, Jesus.

We give you all glory and honor and we thank you for what you're doing in our midst.

I pray that you would give us compassionate and gentle endurance

and perseverance to steward what you're doing.

Would we be sensitive to how you're leading and unified as a team and community? [*sic*]

I pray that you will continue to draw us deeper.

That you would continue to draw us deeper into repentance, deeper into transformation, and deeper into your joy and love to experience our real belovedness in this.

Just now, I pray for Sarah and her leadership for wisdom as she leads the campus.

I pray for Greg as he pastors and leads us strongly with character and integrity.

I pray for Madeline as she coordinates and facilitates worship and is sensitive to the sustainability of those who are serving you so faithfully.

Sustain her.

Jesus.

We want more.

Maranatha.

February 9, 5:30 p.m.

I drive home from our Lexington school run with my two kids in the back seat. My son goes to a small Christian school and my daughter attends a Montessori school. My mind and heart are full as I drive down Highway 68 back to Wilmore. The sun is setting, streaking the sky with a beautiful pinkish gold. Kentucky sunsets are glorious, and this one captures my attention during what is an otherwise a gray February day.

What is more, I notice a cloud bank like nothing I remember seeing, going ahead of me on the road to Wilmore. A dense group of clouds hover close to the road and seem to go just ahead of me into Wilmore. I point it out to the kids. "Have you ever seen anything like this?"

I follow the clouds, which seem remarkably thick and low through the final curves into Wilmore. And then it comes to me from my scripture reading in the early hours of the morning in Hughes, "I am going to come to you in a dense cloud, in order that the people may hear when I speak with you and so trust you ever after" (Exodus 19:9).

Happy tears sprinkle on my face. How unbelievable! A sign of the presence of God that blankets our campus now shows up in the form of a cloud. "God," I say aloud, "now You are just showing off."

The cloud comes and settles around the back of campus, covering the rear perimeter. Later, I stand outside and take a picture of it. The water tower cross rises above the cloud, a sign of the Holy Spirit covering us as a guard at the back, the cloud of God a sign of the presence of the Holy Spirit settling upon us. I hold the image in my heart as a promise that these days belong to God.

Thursday, February 9, 7:00 p.m.

Our circle of stewards meet in a classroom to the side of Hughes. David Thomas joins us, with a few leaders from the president's cabinet. We stand together, hearts full of expectation and anticipation of how God is moving with our students and on campus this evening. More students continue to arrive. Astoundingly, the floor of Hughes fills.

"How is this happening?" we ask one another. No one can answer—only that it is breathtakingly beautiful.

"Surely when we hit the forty-eight-hour mark, it will taper off," we say to each other. How long will God move among us?

We continue the flow of worship and testimonies. Zachary Massengale, one of our resident directors—professional staff who live in the residence halls—preaches a message calling us to purity in the power of the Holy Spirit. I stand on the piano side of Hughes with Madeline, swept up in the worship. The worship teams sing their hearts out, and the congregation of college students and saints sing with hands lifted. The singing swells gloriously. Without big drum kits or electric instruments, the simplicity of music and words washes over us with beauty.

An overwhelming number of college students continue to show up. When a group has to leave, we bless the group and pray over them as a community that they will carry this outpouring of God's love with them. At 10:00 p.m., I text,

> Friends, the revival continues. Hughes will be open again overnight . . . We hope to have staff presence for emergencies and to provide general supervision in case there are questions that arise . . . Please let me know if you are willing.
>
> Ping. YES! I can be there for a few hours overnight.
>
> Ping. YES! I can be from 2 to 4 a.m.

Our community continues to say yes to this spontaneous move of God. I stay late that evening, feeling the music and prayer rest on me like a sweet cloud of blessing. I share in the sense of the belovedness of God rolling over us. I don't want it to end yet . . . maybe another day or so. Such sweetness. I walk home in the wee hours of the morning, after 2:00 a.m., tired, but deeply soul satisfied. My heart has never felt more content in Jesus. My heart sings a song of yes, yes, yes to Jesus.

3
Enough

But Jesus said to them, "You give them something to eat."

—Luke 9:11 NCV

"Blessed are those who hunger and thirst for righteousness for they will be filled."

—Matthew 5:6 NIV

For I've tasted and seen Your goodness
And I've stood in the power of Your presence.

—Todd Dulaney, "Mighty One"

Friday, February 10

The texts keep coming . . .

2:18 a.m.

Beautiful, sweet singing right now. Conviction fell. Lindsey Wilson students arrived. We have some students asking to be baptized.

5:23 a.m.

About 20 people are praying. Really reverent, and God is doing some great work.

6:17 a.m.

One of our students has been praying for her sister from Mount Vernon Nazarene College and that campus—and come to find out a group of students took a bus, and they are on their way.

7:57 a.m.

Ended up staying until about 2:30 a.m. praying with students. Much deliverance and healing. So much good that God is doing!

8:15 a.m.

Mt. Vernon students are here, and they are leading worship.

8: 15 a.m.

Different people have already brought donuts. They just keep showing up with food.

Since early in the morning the day before, people continue to bring food. No one requests food. People just bring it. John Morley, one of our Student Life staff "lifers"—he's part of the fabric of the place—brings donuts from IGA, Joe Bruner, my main partner in supporting students, picks up bottled water and granola bars from Sam's Club. A friend texts me that she is putting together a meal train for the revival stewards. A classroom near Hughes hosts the space for food, but unfortunately, a class shows up to meet at the same time as people are unloading food. I quickly connect with the registrar's office. Can the class meet in another space just for a couple of days? Yes. Yes, yes, yes—our faculty and staff keep saying yes. Two Asbury Student Life team members, Christine Endicott, Michelle Kratzer, and the Salvation Army Student Center director, Alma Cain, set up tables and assist with organizing the food donations and the constant trash removal. I pass by tables in the lobby area with twenty large pizza boxes leaning in a stack on a side table. The receipt is from an unknown "Dan" with a Tennessee address.

During the afternoon, I meet a mom with her daughter. I slide into a row with them for a moment, enjoying the connection amid the worship stewarding and logistical coordinating. The mother is from Indianapolis. She baked chocolate chip cookies and drove three hours to share them with the students. "I have been praying and baking all day," she says to me.

In that moment, what I don't know is that in just a few days the world will come to our door, and people will need to be fed. People will show up with baked goods, apples, protein bars, cheese sticks, a Crock-Pot of potato soup, homemade scotchies, brownies, and a Grandma's Famous Hummingbird Cake. Over the days, Chick-fil-A arrives in batches. Bags of food from Chipotle, City Barbeque, and Qdoba show up. Boxes upon boxes of donuts dot any available surface. The community and beyond will feed all the stewards and students. A church in Ohio will borrow a food truck to drive down to Wilmore and serve meals in the semicircle. With the food they bring with them, they will cook and give away meals to hundreds. Unexpected donations will roll in. A semi-truck will drop off a load of ground beef without request. The church group will cook for three more days and feed the lines of people. The Salvation Army emergency relief team will soon bring portable kitchens to cook and hand out free food to the masses. A local Nashville hot chicken restaurant will give away meals to our students. Coffee trucks will park on campus. People will continue to show up, bringing homemade banana bread and casseroles for our worship teams. Worshippers in lines will share with one another what they have brought with them out of their backpacks. There will be times when we will run out of bottled water only to get a text that someone has just arrived with a truckload of bottled water. The generosity will testify to the abundance of God. God owns the "cattle on a thousand hills" flows through my spirit (Psalms 50:10). But on Friday, February 10, the pizzas, donuts, and Chick-fil-A feel miraculous.

Today as I move back and forth between Hughes and the classroom turned community space for the worship leaders and staff, I notice a folding table set up in the corner by the water fountain with a Keurig machine and a small assortment of coffee pods to choose from. Sugar, creamer, stir sticks, and cups are arranged with care. A student sits in a folding chair beside it, and she immediately stands up when I come over. "May I make you some coffee?" she asks.

"Sure, but I can make it. Did you set this up?"

"Oh, I want to make it for you. What kind do you want?

"No, let me."

She moves my hand away and starts making a cup of coffee. "Jesus told me to set up a coffee station and serve people coffee," she says seriously.

She does not reveal much emotion on her face, just honest brown eyes and a quiet expression. I study her for a moment, taking note of the noise-reducing headphones nearby.

"My daughter uses headphones like those. She has a hard time with loud noises and lots of people," I share conversationally.

"Me too. I have autism. These headphones help me process the noise better. Here's your coffee."

"Thank you," I say, gratefully. I walk away slowly with my coffee, the student's straightforward obedience holding my attention. I feel the Holy Spirit through her, simple and right.

I sip the coffee and go back in through the side door of Hughes. I keep thinking about the coffee-making student and the story of Jesus teaching His disciples in the synagogue. When Jesus and His disciples watched those with great resources make a show of giving, it was to the widow that Jesus directed their attention. *You see the woman over there who has put into the offering all she had? She put in very little, but it's all she had. She's the one to watch"* (see Luke 21:1–4).

Who is the one to watch in this move of God? The gathering has no big speaker or big worship band. There is nothing fancy about our platform. We have no planned or orchestrated publicity. The ones to watch are the students whom God is interrupting in a brilliant and beautiful way. The ones to take note of are all in, heart and soul, surrendered. The ones like our student with the coffee table, obediently pressing into what God called her to do. This move of God is marked by humility. It is not about anyone other than Jesus. I have spent hundreds of hours planning worship services in my life, but this is simply the Holy Spirit settling upon us. I get to be a doorkeeper in the house of God. I get to tend the platform, the seats, the space, and the rhythm of prayer and worship. My heart beats with such peace and wonder. In the economy of the kingdom, there are no rock stars or celebrity Christians. The central figure of the kingdom of God is the crucified and risen Jesus. The position of our hearts in the surrendered life challenges the powers and ideologies of this world, more than the influence of celebrity Christians with likes and squares on a screen. Followers of Christ come from every tribe and tongue, many political perspectives, and cultural landscapes, but it is the gravity of the claim "Jesus is Lord" that pulls us together.

I ponder what God is doing at Asbury and one clear truth unfolds. This movement of God is not about personality, talent, or flash. It is not about outstanding preaching, a hip worship team, or the most engaging communicator. The consecrated posture of the heart, not the rise of talent, the willingness to serve, not the impressive résumé, holds the door open for the love of God.

As we pass the forty-eight-hour mark, the increasing flood of students surprises us. More students from other schools are arriving. Jen Haseloff, Greg's wife, puts together a QR code and sign-up sheet to help students find places to sleep. The Wilmore community rises to the occasion, freely offering beds and couches, food and bottled water. From all sides, people are asking to help, showing up, bringing food, and offering space without being asked. It is stunning and beautiful.

A core team emerges to discern how to steward the worship space for the increasing number of students. We start a rhythm of meeting every few hours. We try meeting in the community room, but it is too busy. We try the back of the Hughes stage, but it is too loud and distracting. We want to be close to Hughes but need space to pray and listen well to one another. We settle on a small storage closet of musicians' equipment behind the auditorium. There we pull in chairs or sit on the floor, essentially knee to knee. Someone finds a dry-erase board, and we mount it precariously against a chair. I write "evening worship" across the top in blue marker.

We begin to craft, hesitatingly, a simple structure for the evening service. Housekeeping items must be addressed. As an old building, Hughes cannot tolerate jumping in the balcony or more weight than there are number of seats. The ledge of the balcony must be clear of coffee cups or Bibles to prevent concussions below. Visiting students do not know how to locate restrooms or where to get bottled water or the housing QR code. We need a time for welcome and house-keeping. In addition, testimonies, and scripture readings seem right. This is the way we saw the Spirit move in the first hours. A simple message of preaching and surrender. An open altar.

The emerging core team comprises a diverse group, including both Asbury and non-Asbury individuals, spanning multiple genera-tions from the early twenties to the early sixties. Men and women, whether seminary-trained or not, serving as pastors or administra-tors—all of us share a common understanding that we are called to steward what God is doing. Regardless of our official roles within the university, the collective sense we embrace is that we will listen to the Holy Spirit together, not relying on a single human leader, but en-gaging in shared group discernment. As we listen together, we com-mit to following the Holy Spirit for as long the waters stir. We move forward as a group that has never collectively made decisions before, feeling a bit like we are in a lifeboat. I feel the emotional tension as we bring our experiences together. In the Asbury world, we are generally a relaxed group not heavily dependent on academic hierarchy but we do report through a structure for efficiency and communication. Setting this structure aside seems right. We are only stewards of what the Holy Spirit is doing. We do not have a church or denominational authority other than Asbury's theological ethos. I am ordained in the Free Methodist Church, another is ordained in the United Methodist Church, and yet another in the Christian Missionary Alliance denomination. One serves as an elder at a Presbyterian church. Another holds deep theological roots in the holiness tradition, and another leads worship and ministers with a more charismatic style. Making decisions as a group is incredibly challenging work even with deeply forged relationships and clear guideposts. What we are trying to do amid a pressured timeline seems impossible.

With my laptop open and phone in hand, I coordinate logistical details during the meeting. I have planned worship services in some way or another for college students for seventeen years of my life. Yet, I flounder now, with all the personalities and perspectives. I want each voice to be heard and valued. This takes time, practice, and trust. We have no other option but to instinctively trust one another and figure out a way to make decisions under pressure.

We share one transformative thing in common: a *yes* to the movement of God. *Let it be to us according to Your word.*

A testimony of healing comes that night: one of our students with mild cerebral palsy who had never ran in his life. His father, a theology professor at Ohio Christian University, drives down to be present for the worship and for his son. On this day, after prayer, the student runs down a sidewalk for the first time in his life. More testimonies of God's healing power emerge. I stand with the student and his dad at the side of the platform, our hearts bursting with the goodness of God. The singing swells, and the worship continues into the night.

The students keep coming. The spiritual floodgates open, and students continue to pour into Hughes. It is a flood of Gen Z into

Hughes and a flood of God upon them. At about 10:30 p.m. David gives a call for younger generations to pray over the parenting generation and the parenting generation to pray over the younger generation. "We need spiritual parents to bless Gen Z and Gen Z to bless these spiritual parents." David's own heart echoes this deep call of the soul to spiritually parent the younger generations. I clearly see young adults are drawn to David's pastoral wisdom and warmth, and his heart turns toward them as a father.

With emotion, the worship team sings out the words of "The Blessing," which seems to fall almost physically upon the congregation, hovering above the hands resting on shoulders and heads in multigenerational blessing.

He is for you. The words echo in my soul for these students. My eyes feel hot and bright with tears, and my heart aches with the beauty and expansiveness of the moment. On the platform, a few students are close by, and I place my hands on their heads and pray a prayer of blessing upon them. I look up to the balcony and see four or five students leaning over Kevin, our president, with hands on his shoulder and across his back, praying fervently. Two of our student government leaders come over to me. Tears well up in their eyes, and they lean over me, praying, and blessing me. A sense of unity of relationship envelopes us. The humility of the moment engulfs me like a flood of honest love and compassion.

As I stand on the stage, present to the work happening in Hughes, the lighting seems to glow with the power of God. Streams of light shine down from above, although it is dark outside, pouring out upon the congregation as a reflection of the lighting in the room or a manifestation of the Spirit; I do not know. The beauty of the sight mirrors the presence of Jesus upon us and touches me. I snap a picture on my phone at 10:35 p.m. Little do I know, this picture will be shared around the world and will appear on the covers of magazines and blog posts, captured as a moment in time with God.

Over the past thirty years, I have walked with college students at three different colleges. Along the way I felt more like an older sister or an aunt than a parent to these students. Now many of their parents are younger than me. I gave and received in unique ways over the years. There are ways that I could mentor students when I was in my twenties whose lives I cannot speak into now in the same way. There are things that I could offer now that I never could offer in my twenties or thirties. Each season of life brings different kinds of fruit. All along the way, college students connect me back to my soul. Their earnest love of Jesus, their willingness to linger in worship, their intentionality to lean into vocational call and dream big dreams of God encourage me. Their love of Jesus encourages my love of Jesus!

A local news story picks up what is happening at Asbury as their Friday night "big story." A reporter comes to the lobby of Hughes and interviews a couple of students for their eyewitness testimonies. It seems both wonderful and weird that these contagious days of worship have gained media coverage. I feel a bit uncomfortable with that kind of attention about worship and prayer. Our strategic communications team does as well. No one invites the media to come, but they try to respond to their requests graciously.

At 1:00 a.m. the crowd is still about 250 students strong. At 2:00 a.m. students from Anderson University arrive. One of the core team members texts a prayer over us late that night:

Give us personal clouds, Lord.

We desperately need the presence of God to cover us. I think of the glorious bank of clouds surrounding Asbury in the evening, and it reminds me of the thick cloud that guided the Israelites.

May the clouds of the presence of God fall upon us, I pray earnestly in my heart. *We desperately need You to guide us.*

Saturday, February 11

The core team meets for prayer and discernment on Saturday morning. We continue to ask one another, "How do we see God moving in our midst?"

We create a rhythm of the day of Asbury student testimonies, open Gen Z testimonies, worship, teaching, and prayer ministry. Greg shares with the team his reflections on the priorities of consecration of the heart, centrality of love in the gospel, unity, anxiety and mental health, and church hurt. We start to weave together ideas for short teachings.

Should we offer communion?

Emily Leininger, one of the resident directors, texts the group. Several others affirm it is on their minds and hearts as well. Communion seems a natural response to the outpouring of love we are experiencing in Hughes. We begin to put together a plan for the bread and juice that evening.

I can hardly believe my eyes as more and more people come into Hughes. It is astounding! College students still come in droves, but other people start arriving as well. I sit on the carpeted steps of the platform, watching the crowd grow, with a mixture of incredulousness and joy.

How do people know to come? The Holy Spirit at work through the mode of social media appears to be the only plausible answer.

Word travels like wildfire across social media platforms.

"Are we going to have enough room for the service tonight?" I ponder out loud to Jeannie Banter. As a pastoral presence on campus, Jeannie carries the hearts of the students in her own heart. Jeannie's sensitivity to the Spirit is a sign of her anointing for ministry. I follow her up on the platform steps. The team alternates on serving as the spiritual authority in the room although Jeannie proves to be the most consistent presence in this ministry. We quickly learn we need to shepherd the space. With so many people who are not part of our community, with diverse expressions and experiences, it immediately becomes obvious that we cannot release the spiritual authority to whatever simply emerges. Our Asbury students respect Hughes, grasp the context of how worship happens on campus, and are shaped by our Wesleyan theology. They know what is appropriate in a chapel context. These new faces seem sincere and worshipful, but we feel a fresh sense of responsibility to care for both the community and this holy space. Almost every seat is filled, even at 3:00 p.m. Jeannie and I position ourselves on the platform, looking out at the crowd, praying, singing, worshipping, being present with Jesus. We keep eyes on the whole space. From the balconies to the floor, our eyes sweep the room prayerfully. Throughout the days, Jeannie's fierce and gentle presence is a supernatural hedge of protection in the auditorium. I rely on Jeannie's constant and steady discernment.

Unaware there are such people as "revival chasers," I learn some people follow movements of God around the nation and show up to experience them. People arrive with their own spiritual experiences and styles from other cultures and places of worship—not wrong, just not in step with how we perceive God moving at Asbury. As the worship continues, a "holy laughter" grabs my attention as an expression of the Holy Spirit. Our core team discerns together to honor how God showed up in those first forty-eight hours as the plumbline to determine what is appropriate at present. Already, staff help people find seats and try to track down streaming phones. I text the staff to keep listening for the "holy laughter" and gently redirect people since it feels disruptive instead of worshipful—not the gentle and joyful presence of Jesus we are experiencing. People also roll out their worship flags and banners across the front, and worship dancers twirl around the stage. Quietly yet seriously, we ask that flags be rolled up and that participants join in worship without dancing.

While these expressions in the Spirit may be perfectly fitting in another worship space, we steward the space in regard to how the Holy Spirit showed up in the first hours. We are both gentle and fierce.

7:00 p.m.

It appears that the whole city gathers at the door of Hughes. Over two thousand people crowd into a space for fifteen hundred. Except for the balcony, people fill the aisles, overflow in the doorways, cram into the lobbies, and cover every bit of carpet in front of the stage. So many people sit cross-legged in rows on the floor that we step on someone if we try to cross in front of the stage.

The sight of the sheer humanity pierces my heart with the immense beauty of people desiring to meet God. I squish into a space at the piano side of Hughes by Madeline, breathing in the glorious sight of the overly full space. Madeline has arranged the student-led worship teams all day with intentionality. What she shepherds today surpasses my comprehension. She knows what it is to worship and to seek the face of Jesus with deep authenticity, leading from her heart with honesty and emotion. Together with her husband, Ben, she cares for the worship teams the way a shepherd cares for sheep. An interracial couple, their marriage reflects the unity of diversity central to our worship. The teams reflect the multiethnic beginnings of the movement of God. We keep the same layout as in the early hours of worship. Worship leaders keep to the side near the piano, with no big drums or electric instruments. Simple songs, repeatable choruses, no lyrics. The singing resounds, radiant and shining, lifting us as one body into heaven.

The chapel is on fire in the light and flame of the Spirit. Joy fills Hughes as though a choir of angels joins the singing. The beauty of the presence of God descends. I think differently about heaven now.

As a kid the idea of worshipping God for eternity never captivated me. With more theological maturity, I realize worshipping God may take many embodied forms, not simply singing in a circle around Jesus. Now as I experience the overflowing love of Jesus in Hughes, unending worship compels me in a whole new way.

Our university president walks to the podium. "Hi. My name is Kevin. I work here." Titles and degrees fade away, and only Jesus matters. With conviction Kevin preaches from John 17, Jesus' prayer for His followers to be one. Kevin has sown John 17 into our campus over the past four years. While we might interpret unity as being nice or tolerant of one another or even having the same belief system, for the Christian, unity begins with a heart turned toward Jesus in surrender. Unity for the Christian is identified by a hunger and thirst for righteousness together, not the low bar of harmony. Not even ideologies give lasting unity; only the affections of the heart ordered under God brings true oneness. In a nation polarized by masks and vaccines, racial identity and political persuasions, Kevin preaches unity under the lordship of Jesus Christ as the only way forward.

At some point that evening, a folded note passes through the crowd to me. I unfold the paper. "I talked to Sharon,[1] and she wants you to know that she is OK, and she forgave you."

No signature. I fold the paper back up and stuff it into my pocket.

I don't remember Sharon or this situation. With no idea as to what it regards, I can only guess a prior student disciplinary situation caused someone deep hurt. My personal moment of peace in God evaporates in that moment, and I feel stung. The last thing I ever want to do is to hurt someone. And yet, I know that in my role at the university and in other leadership roles in the past, I have hurt people, whether from a professional decision or in a personal relationship. It grieves me. I guess this person intends the message to be

---

1. Not her real name.

restorative, but for me, in the moment, it is as if someone has let the air out of my joy.

Lord, I am so misunderstood, I complain in my heart.

You aren't enough, a voice whispers inside of me. *You will never be enough; you must work harder.* My heart grows cold. *You see what happens, Lord? I am not enough.* I remember the note burning in my pocket. The note turns on a faucet of shame, much bigger than the unremembered situation it speaks of, washing over me, overwhelming me with the watershed of my shortcomings and failures.

A team of students prepare to serve communion. Twenty baskets of bread and chalices line the tables at the back of the stage; students distribute the elements in pairs. The river of people ripples out and back as servers wade through the crowds and share the words of Holy Communion: "The body of Christ given for you. The blood of Christ shed for you."

As I watch, there appears to be too many people and not enough baskets of bread. *I won't take any,* I think. *There will not be enough.* Jesus says to us, "Feed My sheep." *Yes, Lord. You know everything; You know that we love You. Jesus says to us, "Feed my sheep." Lord, we don't have enough bread. Lord, I am not enough.*

Feed My sheep. I am enough for you and for the multitudes.

The baskets return back with the ends of loaves and crusts of bread, bits and pieces, still enough for many more people. Suddenly, I need to taste the bread, drink the juice, experience the body and blood of Jesus. Madeline serves me the bread and the cup.

My life is never about me and what I have to offer; it is only about Jesus. My life is given to Jesus, broken, blessed, and shared. Taking the bread the juice, I taste the freedom to not earn my way in this world. The intensity of emotion short-circuits my tears, and I stand, dry-eyed, to the side, listening as the music swells and voices sing. Amid hundreds of hungry people, I, too, need the Lord to feed me from His heart. There is enough bread of Christ to go around, for me and for the multitudes.

Jesus asks us to give all of what we have and none of what we do not. The Lord does not ask us to give that which we do not have. But what we have, Jesus asks for all of it.

My only answer can be yes. I want to feed the people with the body of Christ, but I need that same Jesus to feed me. My life is broken in many ways, but all of me, given to God, blessed in the hands of God, is enough because God is enough.

Late into the night I stay in Hughes, worshipping. My lifelong friend Michelle remains on the stage with me past 1:00 a.m., leaning into the music and worship. It is blissful, otherworldly. Michelle and I are deep friends since a school club in fifth grade. We grew up together, moved away, moved back, raised families side by side, and worked together at Asbury. Michelle is the person I called when Emily was given the diagnosis of Down syndrome just ten weeks into my pregnancy. I remember walking a prayer labyrinth in Newberg, Oregon, where I was visiting dear friends, walking around and around, talking to Michelle on the phone in despair, as I groped in the dark to find footing for this news. Over the years, we prayed for God to move radically within our lives and our families' lives through medical and emotional challenges. Michelle's generosity of heart and service knew no bounds. After forty years of friendship, to stand with her on the stage, looking out at the sea of people immersed in the love of God, reflecting the love of God back on us like the face of the moon, felt like more than any heart could hold. I knew the presence of God was good, but this was more than I could imagine. The comfort food of the Spirit, fed to us from God's own hand.

As I leave Hughes in the early hours of the morning, I notice the coffee station, tidy and ready for the next day. Cups stacked, the coffee pods in a basket, and the student's chair empty, waiting for her to return in just a few hours. This is a living example of the one to watch in the economy of the kingdom. Not the flashy and the greatest who are called by God for this time, but those marked by radical humility. All of us only steward love pouring out; we don't turn on or off the tap. We could only show up, prepare our hearts, tidy the space, and await the Lord. Only one celebrity exists, and His name is Jesus.

Doorkeepers

Better is one day in your courts
than a thousand elsewhere;
I would rather be a doorkeeper in the house of my God
than dwell in the tents of the wicked.

—Psalm 84:10 NIV

Ascribe to the Lord the glory due his name;
bring an offering, and come into his courts.
Worship the Lord in holy splendor;
tremble before him, all the earth.

—Psalm 96:8–9

You are worthy of it all
You deserve the glory

—David Brymer and Ryan Hall, "Worthy of It All"

Sunday, February 12

Our conference services director, Christine Endicott, posts a sign-up sheet for help with trash, restrooms, snacks, and water. Christine is an efficiency expert with a get-it-done approach. Petite, with shoulder-length blonde hair and exuding energy, Christine has a reputation of managing a lot on campus. She immediately puts scaffolding in place to support the influx of college students and others who arrive in Hughes. I breathe a prayer of thanksgiving for Christine's presence on campus on a Sunday morning to figure out how to support our ongoing worship services. With her influence, the logistics team emerges.

Christine fills me in on what happened. The fire marshal called. "You get those numbers under control in Hughes, or we are shutting you down. It's just dangerous." Last night certainly pushed all measures of safety. Christine immediately set about creating a plan for ushers, with instructions on how many to allow in Hughes at a time.

So much is moving and fast. I get a text that the university plumber is fixing the currently unusable women's restroom. A medical incident brings an ambulance to campus. Joe Bruner makes another run for bottled water and snacks from Sam's Club to accompany the unsolicited food. Christine checks through the list to manage surfaced lost-and-found items, required custodial help, and usher assignments.

Eugene Peterson translates Psalm 84:10, "I'd rather scrub floors in the house of my God than be honored as a guest in the palace of sin" (MSG). Another translation states, "I would rather be a door-keeper in the house of my God." A small and growing team of door-keepers spring into action to care for Hughes Auditorium. I create two text groups. One is "Revival Ground Team" for logistics and the other is "Revival Core Team" for the ministry stewardship.

In some ways it seems as though we didn't know we were pregnant and, without notice, a baby is born and requires around-the-clock total supervision. As delighted new parents, we also are gripped by exhaustion and joy. All of us feel parental protection for our students and for Hughes. Whether we fetch water bottles and replace boxes of tissue, drag out trash, or pray with someone at the altar, we share a sense of being caregivers for something precious and priceless. It is holy, tiring, joyful, and messy, like a new baby. Or is it the birth of multiples? I chuckle to myself. Either way, we are taken by surprise.

The surprise intensifies when we see a line forming on the steps of Hughes on Sunday afternoon. "Unbelievable," I wonder, from the lobby, looking out at the queue of people lining up the stately steps of the auditorium. The wintry weather rose from freezing in the early morning to what is starting to feel like a sunny day in the fifties. People gather patiently on the steps and then in the front lobby of Hughes, waiting for a seat. We scramble for ushers to help people scout out seats as quickly as possible. In Hughes people linger in the presence of God, rooted in their seats or at the altar, the wash of the worship falling over them. I can hardly believe people are waiting on the steps to get into the auditorium. Even though we are now at the ninety-six-hour mark, it still feels surreal. I text the IT team:

Is it possible to get a set of speakers on the steps of Hughes?

Andy Miller, manager of the IT service desk, replies instantly:

We can do it.

Another *yes*. IT is willing to set up equipment for the ongoing worship service even on a Sunday, a very strict day off in our Asbury community. Our IT team is a servant-hearted bunch, but we have clear systems for requesting services and tech support. For the team to be in yes mode and go mode for ninety-six hours is another little (or big!) miracle. God is mobilizing the Asbury team. There is not another reason why everyone keeps saying yes.

People do not stop coming. Our small core revival ministry team meets and wonders and prays. The Superbowl will air tonight. Surely people will go to their Superbowl parties and kick back with nachos. Surely students will return to their campuses for class on Monday with great stories but a recognition it could not last beyond the weekend. Surely the families and individuals have work and school the next week.

"We are at the crest, right?" I question again and again to everyone I talk with. Saturday evening must be the crest of the wave, and it will begin to subside. Whatever is happening here is going to abate. No chance it will expand into the week.

8:26 p.m.

About 170 in Estes. Beautiful time.
—Jessica

Thank you, friend, I feel like we are having the "Asbury [Revival]" together. 2 chapels that bring us together in new ways.
—Sarah

I agree! Better than making a committee to plan unity!
—Jessica

After Hughes was dangerously crowded the Saturday night before and with the line on the steps Sunday afternoon, Jessica La-Grone, dean of the chapel at Asbury Seminary, and I start texting about opening Estes Chapel as a simulcast location. Everyone wants to protect what God is doing intimately in people's hearts in Hughes. The flood of tears and spontaneous confession are sacred. We don't want to show it to the world through any sort of livestream. But a simulcast to another space right beside our campus is a natural step.

Estes Chapel is a beautiful chapel, perfect for weddings, with an elegant center aisle, tall paned glass windows, chestnut wood trim, and deep-blue carpeting. As you step in the space, a stained-glass window of Jesus catches your eye at the front of the chapel. While many couples do marry in Estes Chapel, it is the weekly worship services that draw the seminary community. Like Hughes Auditorium, the pulpit of Estes is filled with preachers from around the world, proclaiming the good news of the gospel week after week.

Jessica and I text back and forth about opening Estes.

Who can lead worship? . . .

Will it be simulcast? . . .

Will there be a preacher? . . .

How long will it be open? . . .

Who will be a pastoral presence?

Unspoken, but under our text messages is one big question: Will God be in Estes like God is in Hughes?

Jessica and I have shared friendship for a decade. In the Kentucky summer heat of 2014, God called us both back to Wilmore, and instantly we became soul friends. We overlapped as seminary students years ago but did not know each other then, just as acquaintances. Little did we know as Master of Divinity students how God would connect our stories in profound ways in the future. We now serve side by side in spirit, at offices across the street from each other, each at one of the two Asburys.

A common confusion is that the Asbury Seminary and Asbury University are the same institution. The university birthed Asbury Seminary in 1923. We share the same Wesleyan theology and ethos, but the seminary is focused on preparing graduate students for ministry mostly as pastors and global leaders for God. The university has a mission to prepare mostly undergraduate students for influence and leadership in society, culture, community, and the marketplace. Jessica serves as the dean of the chapel at the seminary, and I serve as the VP of student life at the university. However, we both are ordained and share a love for preaching and discipleship. We have preached in each other's chapel services and gone on long walks through the tiny city of Wilmore to hammer out leadership quandaries and how to parent our children as they grew from toddlers to middle schoolers.

One of the hallmarks of the Wesleyan theological tradition is the freedom of women to lead and minister at every level of the church. Wesleyans believe that the overarching message of scripture teaches that the spiritual gifts of leadership, preaching, and exhortation are poured out on both men and women. As women called to lead, preach, and teach, Jessica and I lean in together to the spontaneous movement of the Spirit that is overflowing from Hughes with pastoral leadership and discernment.

As the temperature drops into the chilly thirties, the line to Hughes curls down the semicircular drive in front of the main buildings of the university. People button up their coats against the cold and wait in long lines. Commissioned as ushers and guides, a few people seek to convince the guests to cross the street to Estes. Most refuse and want to wait in line for a seat in Hughes, but a couple hundred follow the guide across the street to Estes and slip into the wooden pews. The rest wait for a seat in Hughes. What is drawing them to Hughes? Is it a social media phenomenon? Is it a friend's urging? Is it the Spirit of God calling them? Is it curiosity? Desperation? *God is not just in Hughes!* I silently urge the crowd. I catch a few of their eyes, praying quiet blessings in my heart. Who can understand the ways of the Spirit in the human heart?

When Abram and Sarai left Ur in the book of Genesis, they were in a culture in which the stories were of gods who were made of stone or wood, or in the sky and river around them. Abram and Sarai believed in a God who could not be contained by wood or rock, by geographical location, or by human hands. Yet they must have wondered, Will God be where we are going? Will we find God in this new land? As they traveled, there was a cadence of scripture, in which Abram made an altar and found God close in each new place. Abram came close to God and God came close to Abram. God was in the new country. No land or item could contain or limit the one true God. I have thought of this story of our ancient father and mother of the faith, who left their homeland to follow *God into a new country.* As I have found myself at spiritual and physical thresholds in life, I have wondered if I would find God in the new place.

Hughes Auditorium cannot contain God or limit God. God is everywhere. As an ancient theologian once said, the circumference of God is nowhere, and His center is everywhere. We are always in the center of God. Wherever we are, it is the right place to make an altar to God. Just as our ancient ancestors in the faith made altars at each new place, we find God wherever we are. God meets us where we are spiritually and physically. As much as the line of people wanted to get inside, God was not bound to that building. The presence of God is pouring out of Hughes, down the steps, into the line, and across the street into Estes Chapel. Even as the presence of God settles over us, it cannot be limited. Wherever people gather, the love of God descend upon them. The outpouring of the presence and love of God is not about a space but instead about God. Later, thousands of stories will be told of how God met people all over the world in their living rooms, rural churches in eastern Europe, stadiums in Korea, and tiny worship services in Ecuador through the power of media and the word of testimony. God is not limited to Hughes, and people around the world make their altars in their living rooms and in their automobiles, encountering Jesus intimately and personally across the globe even through the technology of a smartphone. The new country is the geography of the heart, not the geography of a zip code.

Even so, the students and others keep coming to Hughes. We get regular reports that visiting college students who return to their campuses experience movements of God's love. Lee, Ohio Christian, Indiana Wesleyan, and more: God is moving and claiming a generation of young adults as His.

Around 11:00 p.m. we close Estes, and everyone moves into Hughes. The singing rises in purity and authenticity as the night moves into the early morning hours. From around midnight until

2:00 a.m., primarily students fill the chapel, many crowding onto the back of the stage, an impromptu young adult choir leading us in joy-filled, exuberant worship. We sway on the stage and sing and cry, the rise and fall of the voices holds us in a space between heaven and earth, full of light and life.

Our ministry team moves back and forth through the numbers at the altar. Jeannie prays earnestly with students. Jeannie's straight-forward love of Jesus draws students to her. An alumna of Asbury herself, Jeannie tells the story of how she came to Asbury kicking and screaming, knowing she was not in right relationship with Jesus, and sure that the last thing she wanted was to be around a bunch of Christians. But Jesus got ahold of Jeannie at Asbury. The Holy Spirit radically changed her life. Now, Jeannie contends for the hearts of this generation, and they know her zeal for them. Jeannie cares for nothing more than for students to experience salvation and the power of God in their lives.

Tonight, I see her fighting in prayer for the heart and mind of one of our students. I observed this student milling around Hughes frequently over the weekend. Disconnected from everyone else, over-come by whatever battled inside of him, he wandered through the chairs absently. Now, Jeannie leans in prayer over him in the front row with a few others, praying with conviction and emotion for this young man. I pray from a distance, extending my hand and my heart. As the night draws on, I witness the breakthrough happen. Joy ex-plodes across the young man's face, exuberant tears, and peace on his face as the Lord meets him. He looks physically like a new creation.

Late in the night, as I walk back home, the sky is cloudless, and the stars are bright. I am exhausted, but also strangely awake. The lyrics we sang all night echo in my heart. I feel held in peace, perfect peace. Yet, even as I reflect on the beauty of the evening, I think this must be the crest. The wave will pass. We will tell stories of these few days when God turned our campus upside down with unexpected visitors and the way God met our students with such goodness and grace.

Monday, February 13

As 1,500 people lift up praise and worship, with every seat taken and a line outside, I am stationed on the floor with a microphone for testimonies. I hold the mic for Gage, a young man in his early twenties, with glasses with clear frames and a black hoodie. After driving all night from Michigan with a few of his friends from a Bible school, Gage testifies to his experience of looking for revival. The electricity of the presence of God rolls off him.

"I have been learning about revival," he begins. "We have been crying for revival in our city, we've been learning about revival, but I have never seen it. I didn't even know what it was, really. I was like, When is this going to happen?"

He continues:

I didn't know it was real. I have heard all these stories. . . . I have heard you gotta ask for it.

I am sitting there like, God I am asking! . . . If Jesus just localized himself and sat in a room, how could we not drive seven and a half hours to see it! . . . I got here and it is silent and I said, "Is this revival, God?" Then chapel starts and then immediately we see people flooding in. And God said, "Revival isn't hype; it is ordinary people who are hungry!"

And God said, "Gage, I am going to need you to go the altar."

And I am like, "I don't want to go to the altar." . . . And worship starts.

God said, "This is revival. Look behind you; do you see them praying? Look left," and I look left, and there is a young college woman getting prayed over by an older woman. And He says, "Look right, young guy praying over an older guy." And He says, "Look behind you." And everyone is raising their hands.

And He says, "Gage, this is revival."

This is revival! It isn't hype. It's ordinary people crying out for a move of God in our generation! What an honor it is to be here! Revival is real! It isn't just a story that we have heard about! It's come. And it is just not come here today; it's about to spread out to the nations![1]

I cannot stop smiling and crying with joy as the crowd responds to Gage, laughing and celebrating with exuberance. The place seems as if it cannot contain the goodness of God in the moment. What I do not know in this moment is that Gage's testimony is being uploaded on YouTube and social media and will be viewed by the millions, and many people will say to me, "I saw the joy on your face when you held the mic for Gage!"

It is Monday afternoon. Jessica Avery, the recently appointed altar ministry coordinator, taught our core group the ABCDs of testimonies, and with this in mind, I go up to the podium and invite people to come forward to share a word of witness, with these guidelines: "We want to hear from several people this morning, so keep your testimonies focused on A—All about Jesus, B—Be Brief, C—keep Current, and D—Don't preach," I explain from the podium.

Following our sense of the Spirit to be intentional about young adults and teenagers, we invite Gen Z to come forward to share a word. While other generations also have much to testify to, Gen Z holds the door of the Spirit open for the rest of us. The testimonies continue every afternoon, stories of freedom from addiction, God's help with financial and relationship struggles, overcoming depression, healing of church hurt, and redeemed relationship with family and friends. Some are stories from students still amid oppressive situations who desperately need God to intervene in their circumstances.

---

1. This was the beginning of Gage's testimony as transcribed from a YouTube video of the event. See also https://www.facebook.com/AwakeningMosaic/videos/656220656193063/ and "College Student Shares Powerful Testimony from Asbury Revival," YouTube video, posted by Caleb Parke, n.d., https://www.youtube.com/watch?v=vlAz6aTRJ-E.

Later, I hold the microphone for Brenda.[2] Brenda's flame-red hair and bright blue eyes frame a sensitive face, and with a quavering but clear voice, she shares her testimony. I feel her body shaking slightly beside me out of the sheer emotion of what she is sharing. Brenda earnestly testifies to freedom from depression and anxiety. When she finishes, I lean in and ask, "Brenda, would you like to pray for those who are experiencing depression or self-harm today?" She nods and closes her eyes and starts to pray. She prays with such authority and power that the very demons of hell must be scrambling back into their holes. Brenda's voice shakes not out of anxiety, but with the power of God, proclaiming freedom over anxiety, depression, and thoughts of death. I wonder at how pregnant Elizabeth must have felt standing beside Mary, who was also pregnant. Elizabeth's baby leaped within the womb at the presence of Mary's unborn child—Jesus! (Luke 1:39–44.) My own spirit leaps in response to the Spirit of Jesus in Brenda standing beside me.

Earlier that day, at about 8:00 a.m. our core ministry team carry our coffees from the student coffee shop, named the HICCUP, to a conference room with a bit more space and a larger whiteboard. A few members of the Seedbed team, J.D. Walt, Mark Benjamin, Brandon "Shook" Shook, and Dan Wilt, and worship leaders Brenna Bullock and Mark Swayze, flew in to support us and join the core ministry team. As they enter the conference room, the sense of relief and support is palpable. Reinforcements! The cavalry is here! Mark, J.D., and I have shared friendship and ministry over decades. The others are welcome new friendships with a shared sense of ministry. Seedbed "sows for a great awakening,"[3] and as an offshoot of Asbury Seminary, it connects theologically and relationally with our tribe. Revival runs on the tracks of relationship, as J.D. will often say over

---

2. Not her real name.
3. See "Sowing for a Great Awakening," Seedbed website, accessed December 19, 2023. https://seedbed.com/asburyoutpouring/.

these days. I think of all the relationships holding the weight of the movement of God either on the ground, logistically, or on the ministry discernment team. The weight of the glory and goodness of God falls upon us together.

The president's cabinet convenes in the Hager boardroom, which overlooks the semicircle, the front lawn of the university. As we group at the windows and look down, we see people in line, the screen set up on the sidewalk, a Salvation Army canteen pulled up in front of Hughes, and a media tent pitched by the front drive. We struggle as we recognize what we are asking our staff to do—steward this spontaneous movement of God for so many college students, community members, and more. Over the past weekend, the Asbury team made an incredible sacrifice of their time and emotional and physical energy. There is no additional money to pay, no bonus money to offer. We do not have any extra resources in our already strapped institutional budget. The emotion of it all fills me with layers of enthusiasm at both what is happening and anxiety about what it means for our community. As we wrestle with what to do, what to ask, and when this wave of people will end, Kevin clearly knows he needs to ask the university leaders, beyond the cabinet, if they believe this is what God is calling Asbury to at such a time as this.

Later that day, an email comes from the president's office, inviting a group of administrators, academic deans, and key staff to meet with Kevin in a conference room removed from Hughes and the influx of guests. Each individual present carries responsibility, such as supporting faculty, caring for students, overseeing the facilities and custodial services, navigating the simulcast technology, or managing the budget. As they assemble, the group appears exhausted physically but alert in Spirit.

Obvious questions are before the university leaders. This is a phenomenal occurrence, yet in direct conflict with normal operations of an academic institution. With no actionable plan to scale or for resources, how can it be sustainable?

Kevin looks around with genuine appreciation on his face. He is a leader known for humility and sincerity, and respect for Kevin underpins the campus community. Kevin is an articulate intellectual, an economist, and a theologian. But in this time, there is not a philosophical argument to address if and how to proceed, only honest questions of what it means to steward this radical movement of God.

"I don't know how to respond to what is happening. I'm not sure how to make a decision in this situation, and I don't know how we can ask this of our employees," Kevin says, watching each face, "but I think this is what God is calling us to do."

A pause. Then, "Kevin, are you asking us to follow your leadership if you believe this is what God is calling Asbury to, no matter how long it will last or where it will take us?" one individual queries.

Kevin half-smiles with the gravity of the situation. "Yes, I guess that is what I am asking. I think this is what God wants of us, but I am not sure about anything. With all that in mind, are you with me?"

Hard-won trust, grown through the last four years of university challenges, permeates the room between the faculty, staff, and the president. No one knows the right answer, but they do trust Kevin. The last years have pressed the Asbury team in every way, from a declining enrollment to staff and faculty reductions and reallocating budgets, but one thing has grown even amid adversity—trust. This kind of trust also leads those present to know that if they say no, Kevin will not proceed. A president cannot command this kind of service; it can only be given.

Slowly, the administrators, staff, and deans turn to one another and to Kevin: "Yes, we're with you." They are with Kevin, but more than that, they also know God is doing something incredible before their eyes.

Later that day, the core ministry team eats dinner together in a dining room off the main student cafeteria. We pull a dry-erase board and the same blue marker from our storage room meeting space and put together a flow of preaching, prayer, and altar ministry that will happen that evening.

David presses us, "What are you experiencing? What is happening here?"

"Revival."

"Confession."

"Repentance."

"Testimony."

"Peace."

"Love."

"Joy."

We take turns answering, seeking to discern together in real time what God is doing.

"Revival," someone repeated.

"Usually something is not named a revival until later, after people look back and see what God did." David encourages us to press into the theology of revival and awakening. Throughout these days, David puts words and vision to give meaning to what often felt completely overwhelming. "What are we experiencing from God right now?"

"An outpouring of God's love," someone else replies. "We are under the outpouring of God's love."

Outpouring. God is pouring out love upon our community, campus, other students, and now even more people. The love of God drenches us, immersing us in His presence. We stand under the torrent of God's love. God's love pouring out on us. Outpouring.

I reach for my phone and find our text group that I'd named "Revival Core Team." I change the name to "Outpouring Core Team."

Immediately, someone texts me back.

So, it's the Outpouring?

Yes, it seems right. We will let history determine if what is happening truly awakens and revives hearts. But we know we are experiencing an outpouring of God's love like nothing we experienced before. An outpouring of heaven.

After the sixteen days of the presence of God that settles like a thick cloud on our campus, I will read the journal from our most famous alumnus, E. Stanley Jones, statesman, author, missionary, friend of Gandhi, and presidential confident of Roosevelt. In February 1905, he had gathered with several other students in a room to pray, and the Holy Spirit had seemed to enter the room and settle upon them. The Spirit of God had stirred among the students, and E. Stanley Jones recorded in his journal that an *outpouring* of the love of God had come upon them. I will ponder this reality of God at work across more than a century. Jesus is the same yesterday, today, and forever. What Jesus has done before; Jesus will do again. That's the nature of God.

As the constant worship wraps around the clock, I find Madeline at the stage steps in the evening, with tears in her eyes. She is running with little sleep and huge responsibility to shepherd the worship teams around the clock, overwhelmed with pressure. Tears spring to my eyes too, my own emotions tight in my chest and in my throat, a combination of exuberance and stress. When Madeline joined the team eighteen months earlier, I had known immediately that her sensitivity to the Spirit of God, theology of worship, and organizational skills prepared her to coordinate chapel. We worked together brilliantly, complementing each other's abilities with an easy way of communicating. We knew how to pivot and how to plan, but this took everything to another level.

"It's too much," Madeline admits between tears. The weight of coordinating all the music rested primarily on her and her husband, Ben's, shoulders. While well-meaning Asbury team members tried to give them pragmatic solutions to scheduling, Madeline's own spirit knew God had called her to guard the sacredness and reverence of the worship. This is not a matter of simply entering names on a spreadsheet; this is holy work.

"It is too much," I agree wholeheartedly. "You are amazing. God is using you mightily. I know God has you here on purpose, but this is too much for any of us. No can stand up under this without the power of the Holy Spirit," As I encourage her, I preach the words to myself as much as to her. We sit side by side on green chairs alongside the wall at the front of the auditorium beside Maria Brown. Maria's close-cropped silver hair frames a steady and kind face. Her spirit of gentle fierceness for God personifies so much of our work as door-keepers. Madeline leans on Maria and weeps, Maria prays, and the worship music surrounds us and lifts us, engulfing everyone in the love of Jesus. In every step and every moment, we need Jesus. None of could begin to do this in our human power.

Zach and Jeannie preach that night, sharing the message of the gospel and the full surrender to the work of God in their lives. Zach's authenticity and heart for the lost rings out, his approachability and personal vulnerability an invitation God uses again and again.

Preaching the power of victory over sin, full consecration, and surrender to God, Jeannie calls people to make their hearts a "beautiful graveyard," surrendered to Jesus. "Let's go!" Jeannie exclaims. Jeannie's "Let's go!" reverberates through Hughes today and in the days to come. "Let's go with God, deeper and further. Come on, God—do it again!"

Death to self, new life in Jesus, the breath of God exhaling onto dead bones and life returning, bone to muscle, muscle to flesh, flesh to skin, alive as new creations in God is a word picture of the work in the Spirit tonight (see Ezekiel 37). While the altar remains always open, people come in waves in response, prostrate on the floor, kneeling, weeping, and praying at the front of Hughes.

"If we had eyes to see it," David wonders aloud, "we would see loosened chains covering this altar."

I step through the rows of people at the altar, toward one girl my heart and my eye connected with from the stage. She looks about sixteen, with pale blond hair and a white sweatshirt and jeans. She sits on the floor cross-legged by the middle section in the front row, her eyes lifted, her hands clasped tightly.

"May I pray for you?" I ask, sitting on the carpet beside her.

Her story steals my attention. She is from Indiana and is having an ordinary day when she felt God tell her to come to Wilmore, Kentucky, to find out about the revival. She got in her car by herself and drove to Wilmore. She shares that she wants to be a Christian and follow Jesus. After some time of conversation, I pray with her to receive Jesus and give her one of the donated Bibles on the edge of the stage.

"The next step is discipleship. Do you have a church you can go to?" I question.

She does not.

"Do you know a Christian friend you can meet with?" I ask.

She does not.

"Do you know any Christians?"

She does not.

I look into her eyes, taking in her beautiful young face and the glistening tears. How is it possible? How could this girl from Indiana not know a single Christian? I find a scrap of paper and write down my cell number.

"When you get home, please text me. I am sure I can find someone in your area who will help you find a church family to disciple you." I start to mentally scan through the alumni in Indiana I know and contemplate how I can find a church for her through Asbury connections.

"Will you text me?" I prod.

She agrees and slips the paper in her new Bible. She is happy yet pensive, as though she needs something else, perhaps a friend or even a parent. For a brief moment, I imagine being sixteen, far away from my family and my friends, in another state by myself, having an intense spiritual encounter. It is hard to envision her experience. "Please, God," I pray silently, "help her know how much she is loved. Give her a family who loves her, Lord."

I wade through the crowd to where Madeline joins the next worship team. The worship teams seamlessly transition even in the middle of songs, picking up instruments and stepping right into the music. We worship together, shoulder to shoulder, experiencing the river of God pour across Hughes.

"You good?" she asks, and I nod and smile.

"You good?" I ask. She nods.

"It's not up to me," she says after a pause. "None of this is up to me. This belongs to God." Madeline knows that God did not need us, but instead, God wants to do this with us. As an extravagant act of love, God invited each of us into stewarding the outpouring, as a rare and precious gift. Not to weigh us down, but to invite us into more of Jesus, more trust, and more joy.

The very words I need to hear. I breathe deeply, knowing the truth of it through my body.

We are good; this is good. Madeline's features shine with the presence of God. None of this is up to us. This belongs to God and God alone.

Around us hundreds of people are encountering the love and power of God. I look above the rows of worshipping teenagers and college students standing at the back of the stage. Gold letters read, "Holiness Unto the Lord." These words root the space of Hughes Auditorium theologically, but they root the Asbury community in our day-to-day life.

Holiness is not a code for behavioral modification or the morality police. Holiness is about being in relationship with God. Sometimes holiness is confused with moral superiority or the geography of moral high ground, but instead, holiness is about the geography of the heart. Holiness is Christ alive in you. To be holy is to "put off you old self, which is being corrupted by its deceitful desires, to be made new in the attitude of your minds, and to put on the new self, created to be like God in true righteousness and holiness" (Ephesians 4:22–24 niv).

Every seat is an altar, every heart is invited into more with God. The place resounds with the beauty and splendor of His Holiness. Come, Holy Spirit. It is the constant whisper in my heart. *Will you meet these thousands of people? You know their names and their stories. You know the place of the greatest pain and shame. Breathe life into dead bones, Lord, and exchange hearts of stone for hearts of flesh.* As Jeannie would say, "Let's go!"

5

Consecration

He came to Simon Peter, who said to him,
"Lord, are you going to wash my feet?"
Jesus replied, "You do not realize now what I am doing,
but later you will understand."
"No," said Peter, "you shall never wash my feet."
Jesus answered, "Unless I wash you, you have no part with me."
"Then, Lord," Simon Peter replied, "not just my feet
but my hands and my head as well!"

—*John 13:6–9* NIV

All my life You have been faithful
All my life You have been so, so good.

—*Bethel Music, "Goodness of God"*

Tuesday, February 14

It is the seventh day of the outpouring. Instead of reaching the crest, as I'd thought over the past twenty-four hours, an inflection point happened on Monday night, and the surge of people grew exponentially. We realize we may be stewarding a national event. Our core group determines that we will not speak to the press or even spend much time on social media. We do not want anything to influence our discernment of what Jesus is doing before our eyes. The Holy Spirit appeared to use the power of social media to spread the word of this spontaneous movement of God. I have no time to be on social media these past days anyway, and I have not seen a single TikTok or Instagram post about the outpouring, but people keep telling me about the viral posts.

The outpouring ministry core team grows, but with growth pains. With different organizations represented and many leaders but not one person in charge, we rely on being able to discern what the Holy Spirit is doing in real time and under time pressure. We talk about being unoffendable. We must keep short accounts, address things in the moment, and believe the best about each other. We must listen well to one another and trust first instead of waiting for trust to grow.

I sit close beside Madeline during a meeting, and she trembles with intense emotion. I know something burns in her.

"From the beginning, the outpouring was multi-ethnic. Where are the leaders of color?"

Just a couple of days earlier, Ben, Madeline's husband and the joint worship steward, brought the same word to us. It is a worthy and right rebuke, but defensiveness rears up in me. We are trying our best to steward this spontaneous act of God with little sleep and with minute-to-minute huge decisions. I have not seen my kids for more than a few minutes, and I am trying very hard to hold all these pieces of ministry, life, and logistics together. A scrap of anger flares in me and then blows out. The Holy Spirit comes quickly and cuts me to the heart.

The core ministry team around the table today is white. The worship team that propped the door open for the Spirit on the first day was led by two black men and several students of color. We held the multiethnic makeup of the worship teams from that point forward, sought people of color to speak and pray, but it had not fully translated to a consistent core ministry team. Ben served on Asbury's admissions team and could not fully step away from his employee role.

The outpouring threw us into a lifeboat of crisis leadership together, riding wave after wave of exciting but almost overwhelming crisis. In the chaos and intensity of the time, we want to be sure other leaders of color were around the table every time we met. With lament and exhortation to one another, we band together to commit to a multiethnic leadership team.

Kevin's message on unity on Saturday night from John 17 trickles into my mind. We are experiencing the restoration of relationships within our student body. But true unity surpasses interpersonal relationships; it defines the church.

"Unity is an aspiration for the world. Unity is an expectation for the Christian," Kevin later will say.

We are under the weight of the presence of God, and unity in worship and leadership is clearly a part of it across ethnicities and in the partnership of men and women, of all ages. In every way the outpouring of God's love calls us to unity and to lament for the ways we are divided over things like racial trauma, masks, and politics. The body of Christ is one body, every tribe, and every tongue before the throne of God in worship.

The hearts of Gen Z stirred with the power of God, and Madeline is a member of that generation. She bravely speaks up to the generations ahead of her with courage, naming one of the priorities for these days. I think of Mary, who as a teenager bore Jesus into the world. *Let it be according to your Word*, Mary said. God used young adults to bear his message in the world since the beginning of time. Why would God stop now?

I step into Reasoner 214, the classroom turned volunteer hub, taking in the scene. Two long tables in the center of the room are piled high with food of every kind. Along the walls are pallets of bottled water, stacks of tissue boxes, bags of oranges and apples, and first aid supplies. The back row of chairs creates the altar ministry check-in station. The altar ministry coordinator and prayer warrior, Jessica Avery, staffs the back row, texting and typing into her laptop almost simultaneously. Clipboards and lists are circulating constantly to determine the altar ministry assignment locations.

At the front of the room, our campus registrar is not doing her day job of managing academic schedules, and instead types at a professorial lecture podium as a makeshift standing desk, not lecturing, but deep into a spreadsheet of volunteer placements. Giant sticky notes cover the walls with all kinds of reminders and information. Volunteers run in and out, trying to find how to help, as well as a constant line of Asbury employees who left behind their job descriptions to manage the crowds and serve in the ministry. Several police officers hover over laptops and radios in the back corner. Christine navigates through the room with a roll of garbage bags on her arm and a trail of student volunteers behind her. The place buzzes with people and energy.

My mind overflows with details and logistics. I find myself at the center of several different teams that are scaffolding this movement of God. I meet regularly with the president's cabinet first thing in the morning, then on to the ministry team, and finally run to catch a few minutes of the logistics team meeting. We manage complex logistics and even questions of discernment all on a text thread. My attention splinters and my capacity overextends. Each group meeting brings its own concerns. In the president's cabinet meetings, we are concerned with our students' experience, how to manage the onslaught of media, and how to respond to the growing mass on the front lawn of the university. When I enter the ministry team meetings, I encounter deep discernment over the presence of God in Hughes and how to steward it. When I join the last minutes of the logistical team meeting, the update is on the overflowing portable toilet structure, the parking issues around the neighborhood grocery store, the blocked intersection, and how to build a better volunteer tracking database. The orchestration of packing our temporary office location and moving to the newly renovated Student Center hums in the background of my mind. One of our outstanding team members, Carolyn Hampton, masterfully coordinates the plan without several key people—like me—to help manage the move. I wonder about how my kids and husband manage since days have passed since we'd spent real time together with any kind of in-depth conversation.

Now standing in the hub of volunteers and the doorkeeper team, I feel overrun with responsibilities and tasks. All of us are extended beyond capacity even as the strength of the Lord supports us and enables us to keep going. I fold my arms tightly across my chest, unconsciously trying to squeeze out my anxiety.

An Asbury team member, Paul Stephens, gets my attention. "Hey, what are you hearing about where this is headed?" he asks.

I grab a granola bar and walk out the door with Paul, my mind and body snapping back into real time. Paul and I pass an overflowing table of lost-and-found items. What began as an assortment of water bottles and Bibles is now evolving into an enormous monster of forgotten sweatshirts, backpacks, children's toys, scarves, coats, and eyeglasses.

Paul and I step out the back entrance and pass quickly through the "arches," as the students call the brick curved openings along the Reasoner Green walkway.

"The staff are really starting to be tired. I just wonder what the plan is. It seems like we need a timeline of some sort," Paul says. Paul is our campus expert on strategy and productivity, so it is no surprise that his eye is on this.

"There is no timeline at this point." My eyes grow wide with emphasis, and I shrug my shoulders. "Everyone is getting tired. I don't know how we are going to sustain this." From the beginning, none of us knew how this could even begin, let alone how to sustain it.

The question presses us at the president's cabinet and in almost every staff conversation. We abandoned our main job descriptions for the last line of "other duties as assigned." Is our mission as an academic institution changing? Is this what God was now calling us to do? Will we steward the outpouring as long as God pours it out?

Our Asbury team shares a sense that God is taking residence with us in a unique and holy way. The holiness inspires awe, reverence, and even a bit of trepidation. I remember how the ark of the covenant traveled with the Israelites and God met His people at the "mercy seat." The mercy seat is at the top of the ark of the covenant, and the Lord declared he would meet with the Israelites by hovering above it (Exodus 25:22). While none of us are so bold as to compare Hughes to the ark of the covenant, we do sense the holiness of God hovering over us, and none of us want to get in the way. "Don't touch the ark," a few of us say to one another with a smile, but with a bit of humorous foreboding as well. We know what happened to the man in scripture who touched the ark (see 2 Samuel 6:7).

Tuesday, February 14, Evening

A worship leader strums the guitar, and someone balances on the cajon and drums. A piano player leads singing from the bench, praise lifting to the ceiling, passing through the roof as if heaven and earth are one. "Come on my soul, don't you get shy on me," the people sing with one voice.

Throughout the evening the congregation roars in worship! The heavens split open with the jubilation of the people. The beauty of worship rises like a crescendo and then falls into awe and wonder.

As the singing subsides, one of our recent alums, Djaime,[1] steps to the podium and prays in Portuguese. Djaime's prayer rings out

---

1. Not his real name.

Estes Chapel and out to the worshippers in line on the semicircle and by the outdoor screen. A few days later, we will see a flood of Brazilians arrive at Hughes Auditorium, and we will look back to this moment when Djaime prayed in Portuguese and the people had heard their language through the unsanctioned livestream. As much as we are trying to keep holy, genuine, and personal what is happening in Hughes, social media is carrying it beyond us to the rest of the world.

As an international student-turned-recent-alum from Brazil, Djaime learned that visa requirements limited the job availability. Sharing his story simply, Djaime praises God that he did not have a job so that he could be present at the outpouring.

As he finishes his story, someone from the balcony above Djaime shouts out, "Here!" and throws a wad of cash onto the stage. Djaime freezes, not sure what to do and slowly bends to pick up the cash, covering his face with his hands, obviously overwhelmed with emotion. Then someone else brings cash and sets it on the stage. Then another person does, and another. In a contagious act of generosity, many hands pass forward money. And not just in Hughes, but outside people leave money at the front by the screen, and in Estes at the simulcast, people pass money forward in an overwhelming display of kindness. Djaime gathers up the cash, unsure how to respond, and all of us share a sense of awe and wonder at the radical act of generosity.

What Djaime experiences on the stage, we experience with the people in the lines as well. When we walk outside, people hand us money. Sometimes tens and sometimes hundreds. A few people pull out checkbooks. With no plan for any kind of donations, we stuff cash into our coat pockets, and when we get back inside, we drop the money into a makeshift money box that Liz Louden, resident director and student activities coordinator, drops off. The box was last used to collect money at the Spring '70s Decade Dance on campus. A week and a half earlier we scheduled and planned student events and met for student support meetings, and now we are organizing a revival for thousands of people we do not know. Mind boggling!

Without coordination, the Asbury Advancement team returns home and off the road, the marketing team stops posting on social media, and the public relations team do not send out a press release. No one creates an online link to give to the outpouring. We do not even have a donation box available to the public in the building. The outpouring belongs to God, and we never want anyone to believe we are using anything about this to make Asbury's name great or use anything about it for our own profit. The whole team shares one heart and mind in this without conversation.

With the numbers of people surging at the steps of Hughes, we determine to set aside the front half of the middle section for Gen Z. Our own students have trouble finding a seat. "Any Asbury student will have a seat. Bring your ID to the back door of Reasoner" we send out by email and texts.

Estes Chapel and now McKenna Chapel at the seminary reach capacity. Great Commission Fellowship, a local church, welcomes about three hundred people who promptly occupy their seats. We are in talks with another church, Mount Freedom Baptist, to be prepared for opening. A screen positioned outside broadcasts the events, becoming an independent worship space. The area at the back of the platform is made available for Gen Z worshippers and accommodates a hundred students at a time.

While worship continues around-the-clock, with the altar open, we program times of ministry from 2:00 to 5:00 p.m. and 7:30 to 10:00 p.m. The ground team pulls a whiteboard from the library and puts it outside on the steps of Hughes to communicate the plan for the day. This spontaneous movement of God is both technological as far as social media channels and as simple as a whiteboard and a couple of microphones.

Daily, at 2:00 p.m. and 7:30 p.m., we remind people to respect the space as holy.

One of us says:

> This is a 100–year-old building. It is sturdy, but it is old. If you are a worship jumper, please be on the main floor. There is no jumping in the balcony.
>
> Also, in the balcony there can absolutely be only the number of people that there are seats.
>
> Be cautious of putting anything on the railing. Your friends below do not want to have a concussion this evening.
>
> This space is holy space, and God's presence is here in a special way. Conversations should be taken outside.
>
> Because it is a holy space, keep your recording short, and this is not for live streaming.
>
> Our team will ask you to stop live-streaming to honor the sacredness of what is happening here between you and God.
>
> Bottled water and snacks are available in the lobbies.
>
> Restrooms are below the auditorium and in the adjacent building and outdoors.
>
> Look for the prayer ministry lanyards. The prayer team has been trained and is ready to pray with you. If you came with others and want to pray with them, please pray in your seats, but save the altar ministry for our trained team.

We learn quickly we need to be clear about who is part of the altar ministry team. With thousands of people showing up with diverse religious practices, which include things like shofars, prayer flags, exorcists, and a confrontational loud prayer style instead of the bold but gentle way we experienced in the first couple of days. Certainly, God may use all these styles and expressions, but our outpouring team has a collective sense of clarity that what we witnessed in the beginning is what we are called to steward.

Ushers include faculty members, vice presidents, board of trustees' members, students, alumni, and local church members. With quiet determination, the ushers repeatedly ask people to put phones away and direct people with prayer and worship styles which do not fit the sense of the outpouring to other spaces outside the main auditorium of Hughes. We also develop a system of prayer ministry lanyards and training so we can do everything possible to ensure that the people praying with others at the altar are prepared and trained and that we can trust their ministry.

We are receiving a lot of national attention, and with it comes nationally known leaders who do not carry our ethos or Christian understanding. I start getting texts about notorious people and organizations heading our way sometimes by the busload. Nationalists and some divisive political leaders connect themselves with the Asbury outpouring. A couple of them on their social media claim false invitations to come and speak. We invite no one to speak except our own ministry team.

A bright light draws all manner of bugs. We joke to ourselves about it, but it underlies the tension of what to do when these busloads and infamous individuals show up. What is happening here must not be co-opted by a personality, social media influencer, famous preacher, or political party. We will not allow anyone to claim or identify this movement of God with a special-interest group or cause.

The team rallies around one thing with clarity: no one is getting the mic. The core team shoulders this responsibility seriously. Not one person will hold the mic without the core team consensus. We double down on our efforts to hold the stage with spiritual authority at all times. The challenge grows day by day as the numbers grow.

On Tuesday night, February 14, a woman waits for me at the side of the stage. "I have a word of God for the people," she expresses sincerely. I study her for a moment, praying silently, *God, give me wisdom.* "We aren't doing testimonies right now," I hedge. "Maybe . . . another time." She adamantly presses me several times. "God told me to come to you. God told me I have a word for the people." "I am so sorry," I say again. "We have a very strong sense that we are not to allow anyone to have the microphone. I don't have the spiritual authority to give you permission to speak." I move away from her, knowing with my all my heart that she deeply believes God has given her this word, and yet I know clearly it is not the right time. She cuts me off as I turn. "God told me that I don't need anyone's authority," she says with more intensity. "God gave me the authority to speak." She loos agitated and uncomfortable. "I am so sorry," I say again. "You don't have the authority here to speak. Tell me your word from God; I can share it with the others in the ministry group." She shakes her head and abruptly turns away, melting back into the crowd. "I am sorry . . ." My words trail after her.

It is hard to turn people away and to trust the Holy Spirit is at work even in this woman's disappointment and frustration. We hear God differently. My interaction with her and others like her demonstrates a microcosm of the conflict between Christians. People do hear God differently. The core ministry team committed to hear God together as best we can.

We are inundated with these kinds of decisions hour to hour. Spiritually mature people come forward with a sincere word from God; pastors and leaders offer to speak or pray. Some people present a political message, prophetic warning, or a call to pray for an emergency or situation back home. We seek to listen well, but no one holds the microphone without consensus from the team. The fruit of this discernment process along with our strong commitment to steward the outpouring as we experienced God in the first forty-eight hours means very few people are invited to speak or pray from the stage. Fierce and gentle. As the doorkeepers in Hughes, we focus on stewarding the outpouring by following God's presence as we understand it. No matter what.

The evening before, ushers located a man in the crowd with a big media platform whose immoral behavior mixed with flamboyant end-time prophecy and erratic preaching got a lot of attention. Several members of the Asbury team followed his social media posts as he traveled to Hughes claiming an invitation to preach. One of our cabinet officers and core team leaders, Mark Whitworth, asked him to leave, and the police escorted him out. To his credit, he left politely and with understanding. We followed him on his social media for a few days and interestingly, he stayed in a local hotel, claiming God did not allow him to leave Wilmore.

Sometimes ushers take note of a bus circling near Hughes with the name of a group that does not align with Asbury's ethos, and then the bus leaving without anyone ever unloading. One student reports to me that several people arrived with nationalistic signs, and a few students greeted them kindly but firmly told them, "We aren't into that," and the people turned and left. Again and again, we sense the thick cloud of protection of the Holy Spirit on our campus. How else can we explain the purity and shared heart of thousands simply to worship?

Wednesday, February 15

The Outpouring Core Team extends—the Outpouring Core Team 2.0—plus the Outpouring Ground Team grows and moves at a sprint. From overnight coverage in Hughes, to trying to shut down the constant lengthy YouTube streaming, to navigating the increasing lines and simulcast sites, the pace increases. Dan Wilt, Brandon "Shook" Shook, J.D. Walt, Jessica Avery, and Mark Benjamin from the Seedbed team, along with worship leaders Mark Swayze and Brenna Bullock, and Jessica LaGrone and Matthew Maresco at the seminary are indispensable for keeping things moving. Through a connection in Lexington, Luke Long, a pastor with a call to 24/7 prayer movements arrives as the overnight prayer ministry host for Hughes. I feel particularly relieved to meet Luke, and his steady (and literally tireless) presence is like an angel to me.

Outdoors, the line management and guest care needs expand. The food truck parks in the semi-circle providing free food, such as hot dogs and chili dogs, for people in line. Gen Z guests receive priority to enter Hughes, and the logistics team finds a way to "fast pass" the students. Bag checks are now in place. Asbury employees are redeployed for revival services and navigate constantly changing dynamics from hour to hour.

Mark Whitworth and Mark Troyer delve into line efficiency and crowd management. David Hay, the person who oversees campus safety, develops a security plan working closely with the Wilmore Police Department and the Jessamine County Sheriff's Office. Glenn Hamilton's unique blend of pastoral care and logistical support undergirds the team. Everything is scaling, and fast.

"Practice the presence of Jesus like Brother Lawrence," John Morley reminds us in a text. A tiny book with great impact by Brother Lawrence in the mid-1600s, *The Practice of the Presence of God* is a personal classic for me. Practicing the presence of Jesus like Brother Lawrence means to be contemplative in ordinary things, like washing dishes, and to hold the actions of daily life as acts of worship. We "practice the presence of Jesus" as we clean bathrooms, take out trash, organize pizza stacks, and search for boxes of tissues.

The worship leader community also is growing. The worship stewards—Madeline, Ben, Mark Swayze, and Brenna Bullock—nurture and cultivate a growing community of worship leaders who appear through relationships and word of mouth. A shared collection of music emerges, a mix of Christian contemporary, gospel, hymns, and cross-over songs. Worship leaders are primarily young adults, many from Asbury, but as the days go along, musicians and leaders arise from friends of friends, and even nudges—they call highlights—from the Holy Spirit about strangers in the congregation. Several times, Madeline, Ben, or another worship leader has a sense that someone in Hughes is a musician or singer and approaches the person with a "By any chance, do you lead worship?" The response they usually receive is, "Yes. How can I help?"

An upper room in Reasoner Hall, adjoining Hughes Auditorium, becomes the "Consecration Room." Since the fourth day of the outpouring, the worship stewards create space for every member of the worship team to be prayed over, not just for a few minutes in a greenroom before going onstage, but for enough time for them to be set apart for Jesus. Finding a conference room off the education faculty offices, close to the balcony of Hughes, a prayer team forms in a circle on the floor and intercedes individually for each team member to be consecrated to God. The music drifts through the doors and floor, like being next door to heaven. In this space, deep spiritual work happens, and the Holy Spirit prepares each musician for the stage.

After a worship leader team member soaks in Hughes for several hours or even days, spends time in the consecration room with Jesus, and is equipped by one of the stewards in the manner of worship of the outpouring, only then may the worship leader step on the stage.

A few nationally known worship leaders show up, sometimes graciously offering to help lead worship. "There's a beauty in hiddenness," Madeline reflects. "My sense is that they're here to encounter Jesus for themselves and be released from their platforms." We continue to move forward with our community-curated worship leaders and musicians. A few of these more famous worship leaders bless and pray for the outpouring worship leaders, hidden away in the consecration room.

With gentle and extremely intentional thought, the worship team members seamlessly blend teams and styles in mid-song, switching out a guitar player now and a lead vocalist in a moment or two, yet staying true to the humble, simple way that marks the music of these days. In a magnificent example of devotion to Jesus in worship with fierce stewardship of the who, the how, and the when, a purity of the outpouring worship shines.

A key leader emerges in the prayer ministry of the outpouring seemingly by accident. A missionary from a restricted-access country traveling in the United States for a few weeks, Mary,[2] is driving through Kentucky between ministry opportunities and feels the impression of the Holy Spirit to go to Wilmore. Mary does not know anything about Asbury, hearing only through social media that a spontaneous movement of God is stirring. She arrives at the tiny town of Wilmore, Kentucky, following the dead-end road that leads to the Kentucky River. Mary stumbles upon the consecration room while looking for a quiet spot to Zoom with her missionary team back in her country and is mistaken to be one of the intercessors. Drawn by the pure-hearted prayer, Mary begins to pray alongside the team. As a mature intercessor walking close to Jesus and through obvious Holy Spirit appointment, Mary becomes the mainstay of the consecration room, a hidden presence who is a vessel of God for the worship team members and the outpouring overall—an unexpected yes to Jesus that blazes a path of prayer around the core of the movement.

The consecration room fuels the outpouring like a furnace. Whatever happens on the stage through the music, happens in the consecration room first. What God is doing corporately, God is doing individually, each person set apart for Jesus, consecrated in the fire of the Spirit, self-submitted to Jesus, a beautiful hiddenness in God.

---

2. Not her real name.

6
The Nations

The woman said, "I know that Messiah" (called Christ) is coming. When he comes, he will explain everything to us."

—*John 4:25 NIV*

Then Jesus declared, "I, the one speaking to you—I am he.". . . Then, leaving her water jar, the woman went back to the town and said to the people, "Come, see a man who told me everything I ever did. Could this be the Messiah?" They came out of the town and made their way toward him.

—*John 4:25–26, 28–30 NIV*

For yours is the kingdom,
Yours is the power.

—*John Wilds, "Yeshua"*

Thursday, February 16

The afternoon sun warms the temperature to above sixty degrees, and many people waiting to enter Hughes carry the winter coats they wore when they lined up in the early morning. The semicircle lawn now hosts two large screens and speakers with a couple hundred chairs for guests who may never get to join the students inside for worship. The Salvation Army sets up a food truck on the semicircle to assist with feeding the crowds alongside the church with the borrowed food truck. There are more portable toilets, more volunteers managing the lines, more safety officers (thanks to Samaritan's Purse), more external media tents, more control gates in place, and more people—a lot more people. Overall, the guests wait patiently, praying in line, sometimes creating circles of worship and prayer as they wait.

Zach texts the core team right before noon:

> The spirit on the sidewalk is eager graciousness. Praying for order and peace as they enter. Really sweet walking and meeting guests.

I catch sight of Jennifer McChord, a key leader in enrollment and marketing, outside the Hager Administration building on the semicircle. Jennifer's bright blond hair and equally bright smile greet me.

"I want you to see what's going on with the press!" Jennifer started working at Asbury just two years before, and we'd quickly become not only colleagues but good friends. After a two-decade career in the corporate world, the change to Christian higher education was both a welcome and an enormous transition for Jennifer. We balance on the edge of scarcity of resources in the world of Christian higher ed with lots of opportunity to trust Jesus. A good place to be, but it takes effort and faith to find your footing.

We bypass the line of people twisting around the front of campus, dodge the makeshift gates on the Hager steps, and briskly walk up the stairs. A folding table with an Asbury purple tablecloth and a computer-printed sign that reads "Media Check-In" greet us. Abby Laub, who directs strategic communication, and a student assistant staff the table with oversized coffee cups in front of them and several legal pads, clipboards, a pile of press lanyards, and a sign-in sheet. Over the last week, Abby, Jennifer, and the athletics and communications team leader, Mark Whitworth, spun on a dime to respond to the onslaught of media outlets and reporters that showed up at

Asbury. While I invest most of my time in meetings between the different teams and ministry in Hughes, Abby, Jennifer, and Mark navigate big-network media with our surprised communications team.

"As you can see from our very professional set-up," Abby jokes from behind the table, "we were expecting the media." The Asbury team did not invite any media or press coverage, and in fact, turned many opportunities down. "Please don't come," the team requested of some particularly high-profile media moguls whose reputations could threaten the joy and purity of the outpouring or shape it in another direction.

"Here's the amazing thing," Jennifer shares as she tours me across the lawn. "We tell the press before the camera rolls or an interview happens that they must first spend thirty minutes in Hughes. We want them to get a sense of what is happening before they report on it." Jennifer's face lights up as she talks about the astonished and warmhearted reactions of the press. "They show up on campus suspicious and guarded, looking for the angle. They leave soft and openhearted. It's truly unbelievable."

Scattered on the lawn and drive closest to Hughes are multiple tents, satellite dishes mounted on vans, light crews, and many reporters. Famous news anchors and talk show hosts mill around, prepping notes and chatting with students and Asbury team members. Most journalists interview students or Kevin, but the communications team also does their fair share of fielding questions. Many news outlets run stories online or in print, such as the *Washington Post, Fox News, Christianity Today, the New York Times, and local networks.* Overall, the media coverage frames the outpouring in a positive light, which we receive as another one of the many "outpouring miracles." While some news writers have a shared faith with us, Christian press members and non-Christian press members alike tend to respond with awe and wonder at what they see with their own eyes. It is another act of God to bring the media to Asbury in person, even if it seems counterproductive to the authentic move of God we are experiencing. Without eyewitness reports, the idea of thousands of people arriving simply to worship and meet with God may present like a farce or a manipulation.

A few weeks after the outpouring, a BBC reporter came to campus and interviewed me.

"Now, what really happened?" he asked, sliding his glasses off his face and squinting at me. "Was the weather particularly nice that week? Were they serving something different in the dining hall? Was there something that got the students all excited out of the ordinary to explain this?"

If you are not a believer or an eyewitness, the idea of a spontaneous act of God, viral on TikTok, with global reach, seems like foolishness. First Corinthians 1:18 framed this two thousand years ago: "For the message about the cross is foolishness to those who are perishing, but to us who are being saved it is the power of God."

Yet for many of the journalists and media moguls, something at Asbury gives them pause and wonder. After a full day experiencing the outpouring and talking with our team, one podcaster and journalist, a self-proclaimed atheist, states at the end of her podcast, "Regardless of what you believe, you cannot deny that there are young people out there who earnestly believe in God. And now, I think you can say [these young people] have kicked off a movement of sorts."

Whether you follow Jesus or not, something undeniable is happening beyond human plan or intervention. God used eyewitness accounts to share the story of the birth, life, death, and resurrection of Jesus throughout the Gospels. From the shepherds in the field, watching their sheep and being interrupted by a sky full of angels, to the Magi who bowed their knees in the presence of the baby Messiah, to the crowds witnessing the crucifixion of Christ, to the women at the empty tomb, the Gospels rely on eyewitness accounts. How like God to not only bring in thousands of people to experience the presence of Jesus at Asbury in person, but then to bring the press to get their own eyewitness account! Even though, in our human wisdom, the Asbury team seeks to steward the movement of the Spirit without livestream and press, the compelling story itself cannot help but be told.

Gipsy Smith, an early 1900s British evangelist, preached, "There are five Gospels: Matthew, Mark, Luke, John, and the Christian, but most people will never read the first four."[1] Thousands of people are becoming the fifth gospel as they text, tweet, and share about the good news of the presence of God they witness!

Nevertheless, the media attention is overwhelming. Someone tells me the Instagram and TikTok views are over a million. YouTube views skyrocket. The Google search trend for "Asbury Revival" climbs steadily from February 8 on in the United States and several other countries, like Brazil and Ethiopia. The more the news gets out, the more people come.

In the ancient days of the Gospel of John, Jesus stopped and asked a Samaritan woman for a drink of water. That woman discovered that Jesus knew everything about her:

> Then, leaving her water jar, the woman went back to the town and said to the people, "Come, see a man who told me everything I ever did. Could this be the Messiah?" They came out of the town and made their way toward him. (John 4:28–30 niv)

Could Instagram and TikTok be the 2023 version of the woman at the well? The viral posts about the outpouring are of the same heart as the woman at the well.

"Come and see. Could this be Jesus?" In this time of hyperconnectivity, social media is our modern "went back to town and said to the people, 'Come, see'"!

The whole world echoes the question: Is this actually Jesus?

---

1. Quoted by Bobby Conway, *The Fifth Gospel* (Eugene, OR: Harvest House, 2014), 9.

As Jennifer and I close the loop around the lawn, meeting the media and seeing people worshipping at the outdoor screens, in line for free food, and holding cups of coffee from the Salvation Army, it stirs questions of awe in me. *How can this be? Jesus, why choose this place and this time in history to pour out Your love so dramatically, first for Gen Z and then for the rest of us?* Getting a front row seat to this movement of God just astounds me.

I also ponder, *What did God say to me in all of this?* In my role as steward, I do not want to miss the moment of the Holy Spirit in my own heart. But as the days go on, my pace continues to pick up.

A friend messaged me earlier in the week:

Praying for you in the midst of the critics.

Miraculously, I do not see or hear a single piece of external criticism or even questioning during these days. The grace of God surrounds me thickly, and with little time to be on social media or to read the linked articles on my phone or talk to anyone outside of the immersion of the outpouring, the Lord hides me. Truly, the Lord hides our core team under His wings, and we find refuge (see Psalm 91:4). Later, I will learn about the theological debate over what happened at the outpouring, whether there was enough preaching and scripture, or if certain theological perspectives were honored or not, or why the services stopped when they did. But at the time, I only know the presence of Jesus and the honor of a lifetime to stand up under the glorious weight of the outpouring of His love.

The world is at our door. With all the attention in the press and over social media, word travels around the world of this spontaneous movement of God. The nations are coming to little Wilmore, Kentucky.

At noon Kevin makes the first official statement about the outpouring, posted online:

Since the first day, there have been countless expression and demonstrations of radical humility, compassion, confession, consecration, and surrender unto the Lord. We are witnessing the Fruit of the Spirit: love, joy, peace, patience, kindness, generosity, faithfulness, gentleness, and self-control.

We continue to seek to discern the right balance between orderliness for our university students, faculty, and staff and our campus visitors—and creating space for individuals to have a life-transforming, Christ-centered encounter.[2]

As I step in and out of conversations between the cabinet, Asbury employees, the president, and the core ministry team, I sense the tension rise in my heart between the institution's academic mission, student care, and the overwhelming tide of people arriving hour by hour.

An email follows to our Asbury community around 5:00 p.m. from Kevin, including a statement about the schedule going forward:

After much prayer and discussion with campus leadership, I am announcing our new schedule for the next week. This schedule is an attempt to recognize and steward this beautiful, historic moment of spiritual renewal while quickly moving toward a more sustainable campus experience for our students that fosters predictability, well-being, and continuity.[3]

The new plan prioritizes Gen Z in all services, and only Gen Z and their immediate guests in the evenings. After much cabinet, logistical team, and core team conversation, there is an action plan reflecting the shared understanding of the priority of high school and college students and young adults as the most pressing matter. Also,

2.   Kevin Brown, quoted in Caleb Parke, "Asbury University Makes Major Announcement on Revival," ToddStarnes.com, February 19, 2023, https://www.toddstarnes.com/opinion/asbury-university-makes-major-announcement-on-revival/.

3.   Kevin Brown, email, quoted in Editor, "Asbury University President to End 'Revival' Service, Says a 'Disruption to the Continuity' of the Students' 'Academic Experience,'" Christian News, February 18, 2023, https://christiannews.net/2023/02/18/asbury-university-president-to-end-revival-service-says-it-has-been-a-disruption-to-the-continuity-of-the-students-academic-experience/.

Kevin announces the previously planned Collegiate Day of Prayer service on Thursday, February 23, as the last service.

The Collegiate Day of Prayer is a multigenerational day of prayer for awakening on college campuses. Each day culminates in a global service of prayer. With an earlier invitation for Asbury to host the Day of Prayer for 2023, Greg serves as the convener of the prayer service at Asbury. The 2023 date coincides with the celebration of two hundred years of prayer for revival on college campuses beginning in 1823 by Henry C. Fish on the last Thursday of February. With the outpouring and this date converging, it seems as though the Collegiate Day of Prayer service, already planned to be viewed by millions, will be a benediction for the services at Asbury. The conversation about whether the outpouring services will be moved to another physical location or simply be released in the Spirit to the world continues.

As I look around the congregation from the stage that day, I recognize few faces, and I take in many faces from other countries. The Brazilians not only arrive but they raise their flags in worship. In fact, they are wrapped in their flags and unfurl them every chance they get. As I pray with someone up front, out of the corner of my I see a Brazilian flag the size of a truck unfolding across the back balcony, and I motion to the ushers in mid-prayer to address it. While we do not allow flags in Hughes due to the sight limitations and our focus on the simple worship of the early days of the outpouring, I appreciate the Brazilians' love for their country and their tenacity to try to hang their national flags in Hughes despite our ushers' efforts. The Brazilians demonstrate an incredible heart for their country.

People travel from England, Canada, Mexico, Ecuador, Chile, Brazil, Colombia, Poland, France, Japan, South Korea, Latvia, Russia, Ukraine, and more to experience the love of God in an embodied way in the seats of Hughes Auditorium. I hear a story of a group of South Korean students who get off their flight in South Korea only to immediately book a flight to Kentucky and reboard to return. Young adults from Tokyo join our students on the stage to sing with the other Gen Z members, many from Appalachia Kentucky.

A pastor's wife from Chile shares through a translator during the testimony time that she and her husband sold their car to buy a plane ticket to come to Asbury and experience the outpouring. I am moved by her faith. When I walk by the lines outside, someone hands me $300 in cash to help with general expenses. I pass this money to the woman and her husband. God provides.

The worship rises and falls in the afternoon from exuberant praise to soft silence and then into praise again. From the stage, observing the room full of worshippers, my eyes search row by row, catching faces, praying blessing over each one breath by breath. "After this I looked, and there before me was a great multitude that no one could count, from every nation, tribe, people, and language, standing before the throne and before the Lamb" (NIV). Fifteen hundred seats are not a great multitude, but it is a flash of eternity. These words from Revelation 7:9 come to mind and make sense to me. Of course, if Jesus settles here with us for a time, the nations arrive. How can we keep them away?

The worship leader lets the music settle into silence. The whole room, packed with people, sits in this holy moment, in stillness. "Be still, and know that I am God!" (Psalm 46:10). I wonder how it will be when we enter heaven and see with our own eyes a physical manifestation of the presence of God. Will I shout? Will I cry? Will I fall on my knees in awe and wonder? Truly, in this moment the only response to holiness is complete and utter awe and silence.

As the silence goes on, I start to feel a bit uneasy. I know that when nothing appears to be happening on the stage, it gives space for other unauthorized worship and prayer leaders from the floor to take it upon themselves to try to give a word or start a prayer time. No one moves, but in my human nature, I give a side glance to the worship leader to see if he is going to start singing again. The worship leader sits on the floor of the stage, head bowed and perfectly still, as if in a deep moment of prayer. I wait a little longer and I start to feel restless. Do I need to move into a time of scripture reading? Should I nudge him to start singing again?

Just when I feel as though I need to act, I hear a voice singing from the balcony above my head to the left. Someone gently sings *Yeshua*.[4] *Yeshua* spills over the side of the balcony, drawing with it other feminine voices in the balcony.

A group of Latina women sing *Yeshua. Yeshua.* This simple melody pours out, quiet and gentle.

The name Yeshua takes residence in Hughes. Yeshua inhabits the space, falls from the balcony, spreads through the sections on the floor, resting on the stage. The voices of the congregation rise, and the name of Yeshua—Jesus—immerse the room. The voices sing out more loudly now, and Yeshua is everything in Hughes and everything in Hughes is Yeshua.

Heaven drifts upon us through the singing. We do not need a worship leader; the congregation leads. When Jesus shepherds the room like this, our only response is worship. The very nature of His presence moves us to respond. The body of Christ sings to the body of Christ, Jesus at the center, the people of God at His feet. We barely stand under the weight of His presence; His sweetness and kindness lay on us like a heavy blanket. No famous worship leader or lauded preacher graces the stage. The only celebrity in the room is Jesus.

In the evening people flood the altar. An Indian husband-and-wife clergy team from London, England, throw themselves at the altar. I hold their hands and without introductions, we contend for their country in prayer. Alternating between English and Hindi, the husband and wife pray for God to move in England as He has in

---

4.   *Yeshua is the transliteration of the Hebrew name used for "Jesus." It is also the name of Jesus in Aramaic.*

Wilmore. Tears run down their faces, spilling onto our hands in our small circle. It is the honor of a lifetime to get to be present in the moment, to bear witness to their cries for their church.

A friend brings a Ukrainian woman forward, and we speak through her translator. We stand together in Jesus, the grandmother from Ukraine weeping through her tears, praying for her family in Ukraine, praying for her grown son here in the United States for salvation.

A Hispanic woman comes to the altar to pray for her adult son to turn to Jesus, and another Hispanic mother and I sit on the floor, and she tells me the story of her ten-year-old son in a mental health institution with hallucinations. We pray and weep, weep and pray. We pray for countries, for churches, and for children. No prayer is too big or too small for Jesus. Though we are unprepared to provide translators, translators appear within minutes of a request, time and time again as another example of outpouring miracles.

A family drove thirty hours from Mexico for their infant son to be blessed. A Christian journalist from Latvia flew to Seattle and drove across the country to experience the worship and report on it. At least two Russian families flew to Mexico and drove to Wilmore. The lines and congregation are a spectrum of black, brown, and tan faces. Many countries, every ethnicity, every socioeconomic status, elderly people, college students, babies in front packs and strollers, people in wheelchairs and crutches—the nations gather in this tiny town of six thousand or so with one purpose: to encounter Jesus Christ.

At almost midnight that night, I notice as a Hispanic family reaches the doorway. Bundled in hats, coats, scarves, and mittens against the cold, the family enters with their faces full of joy, rubbing their arms in the warmth. Grandpa in glasses, mama with three little ones around her and her husband, and possibly an uncle or two pause before starting down the aisle. This family captures my attention. I wonder at the late hour, knowing this family stood outside in the chill for at least eight hours with these young kids. Grandpa's glasses fog, and the children start spinning around in excitement. The usher directs them to seats at the very front of Hughes, since those emptied.

As the family moves down the aisle, the expectancy and delight shine on their faces. The mama unzips the kids' coats as they walk, and the uncles and husband untangle scarves and coats, and grandpa wipes his glasses and shrugs off his coat. As they reach their row, instead of taking their seats and folding their coats under them, the family rushes to the altar, dropping their coats and scarves behind them, the whole family immediately kneeling. Grandpa, dad, mama, kids, uncles, all facedown, foreheads to carpet, hands reach out to touch the wooden altar rail in total awe of the presence of God. I take in their expectancy to meet Jesus, their joy at the altar, their tears, their delight in being in Hughes.

What kind of expectancy of God is this?

The deep part of my own heart ponders this, turning it over and over in my soul. What does it mean to live life with expectancy? Could my faith be this expectant, this joyful, this willing to wait on God for eight hours or eight years?

I want to live like this family at midnight, shrugging off my coat and scarf of the weather of busyness and distraction to get to the altar. I wipe away my own tears, knowing that I want to be full of expectation and joy to meet God at the place of surrender at the wooden altar in Hughes or the altar of my heart even if the wait is long.

7
Radical Humility

Jesus knew that the Father had put all things under his power, and that he had come from God and was returning to God; so he got up from the meal, took off his outer clothing, and wrapped a towel around his waist. After that, he poured water into a basin and began to wash his disciples' feet, drying them with the towel that was wrapped around him.

—John 13:3–5 NIV

Have you come to the end of yourself?
Do you thirst for a drink from the well?

—Chris Brown, "O Come to the Altar"

Friday, February 17

Early in the morning, in the kitchen, I pour a big mug of coffee for me and apple juice for my kids, my eyes still blurry from walking home in the chilly early-morning hours. The kids sit at the kitchen island, eating cereal and toast. I braid my daughter's hair as she eats, pack lunches, stuff backpacks, find shoes, give morning hugs, and move my kids into the van. My husband and I usually alternate the school run—but these days, everything is different. My husband has taken over all the school runs and basically everything else in our home life. Waving as they drive away, I shake off the worries nipping at the back of my mind. The kids do not really understand my absence from early morning until late into the night over these past days.

"Mama 'ome?"

Our youngest daughter, Emily, age six, with Down syndrome, asks my husband, "Mama home?" on repeat over the last week. Most typical days Emily waits at the front door for me after school, watching the street from behind the glass door, nose pressed against it, and when we catch sight of each other, it is pure joy. Emily cheers and claps and comes running. "Mama 'ome!" she says when she sees me, with a smile like a sunbeam.

I missed these moments over the last days, and my heart twinges. I squeeze my eyes shut for a moment to keep tears at bay and grab my lanyard with "Prayer Team" scrawled on it in Sharpie.

I live at the edge of campus, just a four-minute walk from Hughes Auditorium. Our family life moves in the rhythm of the college campus. We mark the seasons by how full the campus parking lots are—empty, it's summer (between summer camps); overflowing, it is move-in season; half-full, it is the weekend. We raise our children at college retreats and over cafeteria meals. Hundreds of students have eaten Mexican-style corn chowder or taco soup crowded into our living room over the years. I bought a giant stainless-steel pot so I can make soup for forty at one time. Even after living on or at the edge of a college campus for thirty years, I really love and enjoy college students. Their open hearts and willing spirits inspire me to live authentically and keep my faith fresh with meaning.

The night before, I pulled myself away from Hughes after 2:00 a.m. Worship grew even sweeter after midnight, and the loving presence of God made it hard to walk out the door. Staying felt almost irresistible. "Just one more song," I chided myself, knowing I needed the rest. A full house remained until 2:00 a.m., mostly Gen Z, singing with their whole hearts and praying with one another, experiencing the body of Christ with contagious joy.

As joyful as last night was, this morning I feel physically worn down and out of sorts. As I walk onto campus, tired and only half-awake, I stop in my tracks and look at the line already going around the block as far as I can see. The campus bell tower chimes 8:00 a.m. and Hughes opens at 1:00 p.m. As I view the line with a surge of stress combined with exhaustion, my spirits plummet even more.

"These people have to go home," I think out loud. The tightness in my neck and shoulders makes a tension headache creep across the back of my skull. These people are going to stand out here all day. How can we be responsible for so many people? What if someone gets assaulted or hit by a car or a child gets lost?

The Salvation Army donated emergency food supplies, but surely not enough. What about the kids and the old people standing on their feet all day? What if they never get into Hughes after waiting for hours? What if they are disappointed? Questions rattle around in my head. My shoulders slide up to my ears.

The sheer energy required to show up, serve, manage logistics, and support others is like facing a mountain this morning.

I increase my pace and text a group of mom friends as I walk with the words: "Everyone needs to go home!" Grumpily, I head across the parking lot to the morning cabinet meeting.

Sarah, will you give what you have? The whisper drifts into my spirit.

I stop walking and look up from my vibrating phone. A damp cold just above freezing makes me shiver in my jacket. The crowds, wrapped in winter gear and holding insulated cups, are standing in small circles together throughout the line with a spirit of expectancy even at 8:00 a.m.

The story of the feeding of the five thousand flits through my mind. The crowds followed Jesus on foot from the towns all around. When Jesus saw the large crowd, "he had compassion on them and healed their sick."

As evening approached, the disciples came to him and said, "This is a remote place, and it's already getting late. Send the crowds away, so they can go to the villages and buy themselves some food."

Jesus replied, "They do not need to go away. You give them something to eat." (Matthew 14:14–16 NIV)

Sarah, you give them something to eat.

I really have nothing left; I mumble in my heart. *I am exhausted this morning; every part of me is so tired.* Even with all the generosity and help, it seems impossible for us to continue to be doorkeepers. It seems impossible for me. I have reached the end of myself.

Will you give what you have? See what I will do with what you have. What are your five loaves and two fish today? I don't ask you to give more than you have. I ask that you give all, and I will do the work.

What do I have? No energy and a rundown spirit. *Whatever is left, God, here it is.*

As I reflect on that morning, I see how God again and again reminded me in those days, *This is not about you and your human effort. I will not ask for what you do not have. But I will ask for everything you have to give. Do you not see? I am doing a new thing.*

I step between people in the line who have hopeful eyes, and pass children bundled up in strollers for their long wait, threading between grandpas and grandmas, and teenagers with backpacks. I note the people from other countries and people from other Kentucky counties. How much love God poured out in these days upon His people! He refreshed and renewed them with the love of a good Father. How much He loved them!

I murmur to myself, "Jesus, I don't have very much to give today. Just the spiritual equivalent of a couple of loaves and fish. But You can have it."

It's enough; see what I will do.

After the cabinet meeting I slip into our core team meeting a few minutes late. The group gathers around a square of four tables, with coffee cups, laptops, notebooks, and Bibles spread out. A constant of our group meeting is the double-sided white board with agenda items bulleted for conversation. David and I co-facilitate the group conversations. I slide into a seat beside him. David's calm presence is permeated with a deep passion for God. Equipped with his notebook, lined with tidy script outlining scripture passages, talking points and prayers for our time together, David thoughtfully engages us with questions of the heart and mind: What do we experience God doing now?

My mind still hums with the meeting I just completed with the president and other vice presidents. As our campus heads into the second weekend of the outpouring, questions of sustainability, security, and student and parent concerns demand our attention. In addition, though, we thank God for the many testimonies of worship and prayer nights at other colleges around the country and the stories of salvation and full surrender to Jesus in our own student body.

Sherry Powers, the provost, relays that the faculty continue to hold class and students attend, then worship when possible. Our commitment to be an academic institution remains central even as throngs of people come to worship. Glenn Hamilton, the university lead on finance and facilities, reviews the facilities team plan for providing custodial and maintenance support as well as budget issues. Mark Troyer, the team leader for advancement, details the miraculous generosity of people we do not even know who helped with financial resources without request. With a truly moved spirit, Mark shares how a man in the line stopped him on his way across campus, eager to know to whom he could give a sizable check to help support the outpouring. Mark's love for Asbury is only surpassed by his love for Jesus, and he felt the awe of God's provision deeply in his heart.

The cabinet does not stop talking about the stories of encounters with people in the line, or those worshipping on the lawn or in Hughes, with a spirit of awe and wonder. Although we serve as officers of the institution, our first commitment belongs to the kingdom of God. Though the pressures mount, and the Asbury team wearies, we know beyond a shadow of a doubt we cannot control this act of God, nor would we want to. We pray earnestly for discernment, wisdom, and strength. The challenges sober us even with our sincere belief in the providence of God.

All these thoughts percolate in my mind as I settle beside David with the core outpouring ministry team. I notice the room feels emotional and a bit strained. I survey the faces, new and old friends, all whom I quickly love and trust, and now feel the burden in their spirits.

We seek for no one to be the one in control, but simply to follow the presence of Jesus step-by-step. However, the merge of pastors, worship leaders, and university administrators creates opportunities for misunderstanding. The emotional and spiritual weight of stewarding the movement of the Spirit of God together, without defined roles and structure in a constantly adapting environment, forces our team to be reliant on God and one another in a way that I have not experienced before in my leadership life. I feel the physical tension in my body over the dynamics of our group: Asbury and not-Asbury team members, assertive and quiet personalities, men and women, old and young, institutional roles, personal gifts, and our human insecurities. At one point, one team member offers to resign from the group, wondering about their worth to the team and feeling the same tensions I feel. None of us can give blessing to another to leave the group; we absolutely know each person belongs at the table. In real time, hour by hour, we build the bridge as we walk on it.

The word *unoffendable* is our password for navigating the complexity of interpersonal interactions. To me, it means we believe the best of one another's intentions even under pressured decision-making and fast communication. Additionally, it means a spirit of short accounts with one another. Insecurities and egos and paper-thin sensitivities do not hold up under the intensity of the ministry. Even with our efforts to surrender to one another, to put the other above our own interests, and to be unoffendable, hurt happens. Some things need to be settled around the table.

One person voices uncertainty about their role in the group. Another feels that decisions happen too quickly or without the full group's input. Natural fissures occur between us in the pace of discernment and conversation under pressure. Amid our heart posture to be unoffendable, we need to care for the cracks.

Instinctively, conference room chairs are altars and knees slide to the floor. Some fall on their faces in prayer to confess and clear any obstacle to the unity in our group. Another person is stretched on the carpet, weeping. My forehead touches the table, and I open my palms. *Holy Spirit, come.*

The confessions clear our souls in time. Several people share personal hurts from the group. The team weeps together, and the humble words "I am so very sorry" begin to mend gaps.

With my own head buried in my arms, I cry for the day-to-day pressure we experience together, for my own exhaustion and disconnection from family life, for the misunderstandings, for my own needs to be seen and known. Self-interest flares. I hold a leadership role in the university, and my nature is to take responsibility for others. My ego rises up. Does anyone look out for me and my interests? Am I always just a caregiver for everyone else? The depth of my frustration surprises me. No wonder I am so exhausted this morning. Everything stacks up.

I realize as I listen to others that I do not know how to separate my own complexity of emotions enough to speak it out in the group. The struggle of when to yield to others and when to lead makes me feel tight and brittle, always trying to get it right instead of leaning into the freedom and joy of the Spirit. I pray, "God, give me Your guidance and wisdom. I don't even know how to put words to my feelings."

Author and priest Tish Harrison Warren spoke in our chapel the year before. At the close of her talk, she said, "The door to the Christian life is cruciform in shape." Kevin Brown weaves this idea into our community conversation. We are called to be a cruciform community, surrendered to Jesus and to one another. What brings us together is the cross of Jesus, laying down our insecurities and fears at the feet of our Savior.

As a middle schooler, I memorized the book of Philippians, and Philippians 2 shaped my theology and practice of leadership: "In humility value others above yourselves. . . . In your relationships with one another, have the same mindset as Christ Jesus: Who, being in very nature God, did not consider equality with God something to be used to his own advantage; rather, he made himself nothing by taking the very nature of a servant. . . . He humbled himself by becoming obedient to death—even death on a cross!" (vv. 3–7). The words echo in my heart. Radical humility marks these days of the outpouring. From the platform to the conference room, the leader is Jesus. But living into the cruciform life together under rapid change stretches me in every way, and deep places of insecurity and even anger move in my soul.

I wonder how to bring my gifts of leadership and yet also how to give others space to lead. Is it possible to follow not the strongest voice in the room but to follow the quiet voice of Jesus? How am I willing to be fully who I am with vulnerability and honesty, yet be responsible to support others?

After a time of prayer over one another, a stillness falls. We commit to be unoffendable, not just in word, but by seeking the same mind as Jesus, who put others above himself. We are receiving a flash course in cruciform leadership. The course of leadership lessons both invigorates me and presses me to grow. The Spirit of God pours into the cracks of my heart like hot honey and oil, burning with a refining fire searing as it heals. This must be what growth feels like.

As the confession concludes and a sense of peace lingers with us, I gaze out the window, looking across Reasoner Green on one side of the conference room, the lawn space at the center of campus. While the lines of people are not far away, the buildings block sight of the crowd. The line curls around the perimeter of the campus. From where I observe the Green, students come to and from class with backpacks and water bottles, greeting one another and hurrying to their academic buildings or returning to their residence halls. It might be any February day.

On the other side of the conference room, a window overlooks a large multipurpose auditorium filled with students, quiet and reflective. Over the last couple of days, our resident directors, Emily Leininger, Zachary Massengale, Matt Penny, Liz Louden, and Laura Haugen, created the "Abide" space. Low lighting, circles of chairs, tables with puzzles, fuzzy carpets to nap on, and a table overflowing with food creates space for college students to reflect and rest. Some of our students articulate feelings of being displaced from the outpouring as the crowds come. Try as we do to reserve seats and prioritize Gen Z, the sheer numbers of people overwhelm the student body. Abide gives a place of rest and a place to process. Faculty and pastors join students for open-ended conversation and prayer. The outpouring is freeing to many students, but other students mentioned layers of negative feelings about the crowds even as they recognize the presence of God. We all tremble with both the intensity of the goodness of God and the challenges of finding our way with thousands of welcome but uninvited guests.

Along with the Abide room, James Ballard at the Word Gospel Student Center, David Schnake at the One Mission Society Student Center, and Majors Paul and Alma Cain at the Salvation Army Student Centers open their doors, their space, and their time to shepherd students through the confusing emotions and through this unique spiritual experience.

I pack up my bag and wander back over to Hughes, walking more slowly than before, turning over the time of confession, our group, and the pressures of planning and decision-making in my mind. God does not give us a map of what to do or a manual of how to steward a spontaneous movement of God. Instead, God gives us His presence. I remember how the Israelites left Egypt not with a strategic plan and a GPS, but with the presence of God in a cloud by day and a pillar of fire by night. "Keep me close to the Presence," I pray as I breathe.

In the afternoon Greg invites members of Gen Z to read a life scripture from the pulpit. These Gen Z voices reading the Word root our worship through the hours in scripture, but also serve as a reminder: God started this work in young adults.

Maria Brown follows Greg up onto the stage and takes the mic. Opening her hands, she intercedes for this generation. Maria prays earnestly against the distraction of phones and media. She calls upon the power of God to win this generation, and the waters of the Spirit stir in the room; hands lifting to heaven. The power of God flows through Maria and washes across the altar, flowing through the rows. As Maria prays, she gets on her knees and bows before God, and the congregation follows her example. Silence engulfs the space, and a holy awe explodes noiselessly upon us.

I kneel in the silence, my face pressing the carpet, listening to more than a thousand people be quiet. I came to the end of myself today. My emotions tangle up in my human exhaustion and the growth pains of my heart in ministry and leadership. Now, I turn my heart to Jesus again, seeking surrender.

In the evening, a glorious cross of sapphire blue and a heavenly sphere with gold power emanating down the cross radiates with color and beauty on the stage. To me, it reflects the presence of the Spirit of God, vividly dividing light and dark before our eyes. This wooden cross has graced the stage since February 8. Plain, it is just two pieces of wood roughly nailed together. But a couple days before, a retired art professor asked if he could make the cross beautiful. I quickly agreed, and later he brought it back, leaning the cross against the organ, a representation of the surrender of Christ and the intersection of humanity and holiness in glorious color.

Jesus emptied himself, taking the very nature of a servant, and became obedient to death, even death on a cross. Radical humility marked Jesus. The authority of Jesus did not come from the power He wielded, but from the power He released. As any one of us steward the lavish outpouring of the love of Jesus, the only way is through submission to Jesus and submission to one another. The signposts of the kingdom of God are a basin, a towel, and a cross.

As the evening unfolds, I meet a group from a church in San Diego who share enthusiastically the growth of their church plant and that they hope God will move in California in this way. Their love for their church and their passion to see it grow inspire me.

I also meet a group of men who have driven from Hamilton, Ontario, in Canada. Their stories of miracles on the way down and their excitement about their experience in Wilmore bless me tremendously. As we exchange introductions, I share that I was born in Toronto. The Hamilton contingent celebrate our shared heritage! This forges our connection, and we circle and pray for one another and for God to move. The leader, Solomon Ikhuiwu, exhorts and encourages me. Little do I know that in a few months, I will bring a team from Asbury to be present in prayer for their city with several churches and meet amazing people of faith. We encounter hundreds of groups of travelers over the days, all with a story of how God called them and brought them to experience His presence.

I stay late into the night, soaking in the love of God, enjoying the many worshippers from around the world who want to connect, pray, and celebrate the goodness of God. I also know more and more clearly that when I come to the end of myself, I may truly begin in God. I am not enough, and this truth leads me to Jesus who knows humility and sacrifice. The radical humility of Jesus reflects the infinite love of God.

8
Revival Full

When Jesus saw him lying there and learned that he had been in this
condition for a long time, he asked him,
"Do you want to get well?"

—*John 5:6 NIV*

What a powerful name it is . . .
The name of Jesus Christ my King.

—*Ben Fielding and Brooke Ligertwood, "What a Beautiful Name"*

Saturday, February 18

The numbers surge on the second Saturday. We estimate that twenty thousand people arrive in Wilmore. Getting into and out of Wilmore becomes almost impossible. Officials discuss classifying Wilmore as a disaster zone. Police reroute traffic in and out of Wilmore to deal with the vehicles. Cars park everywhere, blocking exits and driveways. The Wilmore Free Methodist Church runs a shuttle from their parking lot to the end of the line. Fields transform into parking lots. Business owners lend us stanchions, chairs, and trash cans. Another Salvation Army canteen appears. Hughes, Estes, McKenna, the seminary gym, Great Commission Fellowship, and Mount Freedom Baptist Church are bursting with worshippers.

Mark Whitworth navigates the creation of a large screen venue on the semicircle lawn, which emerges as its own unique place of worship. Mark possesses an unusual combination of big-group management with a history of leadership in the SEC (Southeastern Conference) and media expertise. Now drawing on decades of big press and event experience, Mark shepherds the chaos of people outside. Thousands of people experience Jesus on the grass; many never actually enter Hughes. The outdoor seats shift into altars, the grass a place of surrender.

Our little city of six thousand churns with thousands more people. The mayor calls Kevin with support but also with the awareness that the city infrastructure won't handle the onslaught of people. The city sewer system may not maintain the masses of people if this outpouring continues. Police set up a flashing sign where the roads merge coming into Wilmore: REVIVAL FULL. REVIVAL AT CAPACITY.

The nine-hour-long line stretches one and a half miles from Hughes to the Luce Physical Center on the hill. Thousands of people worship on the lawn of the outdoor venue over the course of the day.

I take a seat on the steps of the stage with Jerry Coleman, a steady and kind presence in Hughes, to "hold the stage," fulfilling our role to prevent anyone from taking the mic out of turn. Jerry serves with the Francis Asbury Society in Wilmore, and several of its ministry team, including Kelly and Josh Hallahan, serve faithfully during the outpouring. Jerry and I move to make way for Zach to come up to the stage as the music quiets then fades away.

In the spirit of 2 Chronicles 7:14, Zach exhorts the people to humble themselves before God. "If my people, who are called by my name, will humble themselves and pray and seek my face and turn from their wicked ways, then I will hear from heaven, and I will forgive their sin and will heal their land" (NIV).

People slide out of their folding seats and turn around, making their chairs into altars. People kneel in the aisles and in rows before the altar. Outside on the lawn, people drop to their knees, faces in the grass. As we kneel, shoulder to shoulder, a holy silence descends from heaven.

Again I am reminded that when we meet Jesus face-to-face, we may shout and celebrate, but perhaps it is more likely we will be in awe in a holy silence as *kairos* (eternal time) and *chronos* (clock time) merge as a confluence of two immense rivers.

Someone snaps a picture of the people kneeling on the semicircle lawn on February 18, and it is a picture I return to again and again. In many ways, the sea of people falling on their face before God, calling upon His name, defines the outpouring.

Later, I hold the mic for a young woman sharing a vision of the rivers of God flowing out of His temple and into the world. Everything the rivers touch begin to flourish. It reminds me of the vision of Ezekiel 47, in which waters spring forth from the temple and converge into a river too wide and deep to cross: "Fruit trees of all kinds will grow on both banks of the river. Their leaves will not wither, nor will their fruit fail. Every month they will bear fruit, because the water from the sanctuary flows to them. Their fruit will serve for food and their leaves for healing (v. 12 NIV)."

My heart burns within me. *May it be so. May the fruit of this river of God bring sustenance and healing for the nations.* Whatever is happening here at Asbury is for the sake of the world.

Many years ago, I walked past a creek swirling with the rains of the night before. The creek flooded over its boundaries and into the road. The water mesmerized me, the power of the water, how it swirled and churned and threatened everything in its wake. God spoke to me about my life being like a swampland—energies going every direction without boundaries. He called me to be a river, my energies focused, instead of a watery swamp of distraction. Now in the current, the river of God bestows fruitfulness upon the nations through the outpouring of His love. The presence of Jesus flows upon us from the sanctuary of His spirit, beyond Wilmore, to the world. I imagine the fruit of His presence flourishing. My own calling and direction from God all those years ago are swept up in this experience now.

Several other young adults express their commitment to Jesus and the faithfulness of God in their lives through things like addiction and depression. A student talks about loss of relationship through a crisis in her church. A teenager provides a testimony of victory over suicidal ideation and depression. Stories about freedom from self-harm, suicidal ideation, anxiety, and depression often dominate the testimony time. Freedom. God gives freedom. Freedom from sin, freedom from self-harm, freedom from broken relationships, and even freedom from addictions to pornography and drugs. Daily we offer the congregation an opportunity to respond to the witness of life transformation.

Today I sense God moving and say, "I don't want anyone to miss the moment. But this is not a hard sell. This is not your last opportunity to follow Jesus. If today is the day, and you are feeling the nudge of the Holy Spirit, this is your moment. You didn't know it, but today heaven is throwing a party in your honor! If you want to follow Jesus for the first time, please stand!"

A few people rise to their feet, and then a few more. People cheer and clap and hug. The goodness of God engulfs us again and again. I lead them in a confessional prayer together, all new believers standing. The crowd explodes in joy and applause on all sides. We meet the new believers at the altar and pray over them, sealing this new decision in the Spirit. Over the course of the sixteen days, we estimate more than four hundred first-time commitments to Jesus.

I do not stop smiling. My heart leaps in praise. I have never felt so alive in my faith and my call. The delight of the Holy Spirit is palpable. As the crowd celebrates, I rub away joyful tears and kneel beside a new believer and pray over her, asking God to seal the work with His Spirit.

Church, Jesus says to us: *Feed my sheep.*

Yes, Lord.

Lord, You know everything; You know that we love You.

Jesus says to us: Feed my sheep.

We feed the sheep with the body of Christ, given for the world and given for us. The tide of faith rose for many in those days. I recognize my own complacency and unwillingness to offer the bread of life to hungry people all the time. How can it be that I miss the moment to offer the best gift of all time? I wonder at the crowds of spiritually hungry people and the Gospels coming to life before our eyes. Jesus felt compassion for the crowds, who were like sheep without a shepherd. He taught them and healed them. Jesus is the same as He was in the days he walked in Galilee and met the crowds. He keeps doing what He always does, feeding the hearts and souls, healing faith, and redeeming sin.

People long for Jesus. Just as the crowds sought Him out in Galilee, people seek Jesus out now.

Jesus is not casual about faith. Following Jesus is not a hobby or a lifestyle choice. People do not fall on their knees desperate for a moral code. People fall on their knees out of their great need. The longing for Jesus overtakes us. It is freedom, healing, abundance, joy, and surrender. This life of Jesus is a holy way, filled up with God, chains of sin shrugged off and left behind. The desire for sin transforms into a hunger for righteousness.

Jesus invites us to life that redefines everything about us—our instincts and our loves, our priorities, and our most internal motivations. The call of Jesus is to give your life away. It is not more of the American dream; it is less. The insatiable appetite for entertainment and prosperity of the world now tastes like sawdust in our mouths.

Instead, the fragrance of covenant, commitment, and community make us long for the feast of the kingdom. Ephesians 5:1 exhorts us to walk in the way of love, just as Christ loved us and gave himself up for us as a fragrant offering and sacrifice to God. The sacrifice of Jesus compels us; the love of Jesus keeps us.

When we surrender all of ourselves, Jesus leads us through a cross-shaped door, which reshapes our lives. The call of Jesus is "Come and have life and have it abundantly" and it is also "Come and die." Die to self, die to the old ways of putting life together, die to the striving and the earning our worth, and rely on the sacrifice and love of Jesus to define us.

In a world of excess and famine, Jesus feeds His sheep the only thing that will satisfy: the body of Christ, given for the world. In these days we feasted on Christ; we lingered over Him; we followed Gen Z, who had pulled their seats up to the table first.

It is never too late. The invitation is yours; the table is set; the party is for you and for me. The kingdom of God is here.

That evening, the Asbury Gospel Choir and the Kentucky State Gospel Choir merge on the stage to shepherd us in worship with Ben's leadership. Hughes grows increasingly full of Gen Z after 11:00 p.m., and the place roars in worship, the front sections of young adults jumping in praise, the stage vibrating with youth dancing and singing their hearts out. The exuberance seems as if it might take the roof off; the place not able to hold the energy of the people. Hughes explodes in praise. "Hell lost another one!" the crowd booms, "I am free!"[1]

WhatsApp Thread

[2/18/23, 7:08:46 AM] Maria Brown: I'm here for a shift in the CLC but I need someone to unlock the door and let me in

[2/18/23, 7:11:57 AM] Christine Endicott: We have a ring in lost and found. She can contact Pam Anderson and describe it to see if a match.

---

1. Dante Bowe et al., "I Thank God," track 7 on *Move Your Heart*, Maverick City Music, 2020, EP.

[2/18/23, 9:18:24 AM] Sarah: 10:30 am logistics meeting in Reasoner 214

[2/18/23, 9:19:18 AM] Andy Miller: I don't think there will be anyone from my team there so if you need information let me know!

[2/18/23, 9:30:23 AM] Maria Brown: What is needed now? I'm available.

[2/18/23, 9:36:25 AM] Michelle Kratzer: It sounds like there will be some cleaning in Hughes at 10.

[2/18/23, 9:37:02 AM] Christine Endicott: Cleaning Hughes.

[2/18/23, 9:37:06 AM] Michelle Kratzer: Andy, I will take notes with you in mind.

[2/18/23, 10:13:30 AM] Jennifer McChord: Are there one or two people who could come to Hager and help Abby and I for a few minutes?

[2/18/23, 10:21:08 AM] Michelle Kratzer: Sending 3—including David Swartz

[2/18/23, 10:48:03 AM] Michelle Kratzer: Could we use the old Intercessory prayer room for lost and found IF WE STAFF IT?

[2/18/23, 10:53:19 AM] Michelle Kratzer: We are doing it.

[2/18/23, 11:06:35 AM] Christine Endicott: Please contact anyone you know at local churches and let them know we are not accepting any NEW volunteers. We are inundated.

[2/18/23, 11:19:25 AM] Christine Endicott: Have a terminally ill woman on steps who is not doing well. Can prayer team or someone please advise?

[2/18/23, 11:28:48 AM] Maria Brown: Can we get someone to pray for her and allow her to go home?

[2/18/23, 11:29:48 AM] Michelle Kratzer: I'm going to find a prayer team member.

[2/18/23, 11:29:55 AM] Michelle Kratzer: Let me know if somebody else arrives.

[2/18/23, 11:31:58 AM] Matthew Maresco: Anyone got another drone shot?

[2/18/23, 11:32:42 AM] Michelle Kratzer: Sending Lyndsey your way.

[2/18/23, 11:33:46 AM] Christine Endicott: See bearded guy with tan coat.

[2/18/23, 11:34:37 AM] Maria Brown: Do we need any more security volunteers?

[2/18/23, 11:35:23 AM] Michelle Kratzer: Not if they are a new volunteer. We're full. Tell them, "THANK YOU!"

[2/18/23, 11:39:14 AM] Jennifer McChord: We are on it.

[2/18/23, 11:41:39 AM] Maria Brown: Someone in the line not connected with us handing out pamphlets. Do I ask questions do something?

[2/18/23, 11:46:16 AM] Mark Troyer: Say no. No advertising at all

[2/18/23, 11:49:37 AM] Michelle Kratzer: There is preaching going on out in the line. Is that us?

[2/18/23, 11:49:58 AM] Sarah: No. Shut down the preaching. Safety officer to help?

[2/18/23, 11:50:20 AM] Michelle Kratzer: I need someone else to do it. I'm in the volunteer room.

[2/18/23, 11:51:49 AM] Christine Endicott: I am going.

[2/18/23, 11:52:34 AM] Sarah: Preaching in the line is not permitted on our property.

[2/18/23, 11:55:07 AM] Christine Endicott: Have not found them yet.

[2/18/23, 12:10:37 PM] Christine Endicott: Line to WGM no preacher found.

[2/18/23, 12:11:55 PM] Jessica LaGrone: There was preaching outside Estes earlier. May die down as lines start to move.

[2/18/23, 12:28:25 PM] Michelle Kratzer: Can someone come and do communion in the line?

[2/18/23, 12:35:44 PM] Christine Endicott: Am I clear to start bag check?

Late into the night I walk home singing "I am free! I am free!" as I cross the quiet campus in the cold early-morning hours. When I arrive home, too keyed up to sleep, images of the day pounding through my mind, I open Facebook, the words tumbling out of me, and start to type:

Day 10

Wilmore community—I am undone by your service. You are holding with such patience the inconvenience of the crowds, the crazy parking, and the sheer press of humanity.

So much gratitude. Most of the people coming have no idea that their usher navigating the wheelchair through the rain has a Ph.D. and their prayer minister is a retired seminary professor. Most of the people don't know how huge numbers of you have set aside your jobs, your family time, and your sleep to show up and direct people, check bags, and sometimes set aside your preference in musical style to be up late into the night in prayer.

Many of you could preach and teach as you have done around the world and on the Asbury campuses. Yet you are so humble to take out the trash and stand out in the cold to get people inside. You have offered to do what you can, and it has been loaves and fishes.

We will never be the same.

Everyone—I was wrecked last night for the people. On the ground here, we haven't had a lot of time to process or theologize or get our minds and hearts around all that is happening.

But what I do know is:

People are desperately hungry to experience God. So hungry, that they pile their small children in a van and drive across the country and stand for hours in a line in the cold.

So hungry, that they are arriving from Brazil, Mexico, Poland, South Korea, Canada, Kenya, Ireland, England, and more, changing their plans, showing up after traveling for over a day, wanting to experience God here, sometimes speaking little or no English.

So hungry, that they wait for hours in freezing temperatures because they want to be at the altar.

As I look out over the crowd in Hughes, I see and hear broken-down people, small children, people in wheelchairs, young people with stories of addiction, moms who are crying over their children in rehab, and shining faces who want so badly to see Jesus and who seem to be deeply experiencing an outpouring of the love of God.

Every generation, every socio-economic class, every ethnicity that's what I see.

Last night I walked down the wait line (trying to persuade people to go to the warm simulcast sites), and I am totally wrecked by their need for God.

By my need for God.

I write this in tears, overwhelmed that God would do a work here in front of my eyes.

As I hit Post, tears course down my cheeks, my hands shake from exhaustion and emotion.

9

Do Not Be Afraid;
Just Believe

*While Jesus was still speaking, some people came from the house of Jairus,
the synagogue leader." Your daughter is dead," they said. "Why bother the
teacher anymore?" Overhearing what they said, Jesus told him," Don't be
afraid; just believe." . . . He took the child's father and mother and the
disciples who were with him and went in where the child was. He took
her by the hand and said to her, "Talitha koum!" (which means "Little
girl, I say to you, get up!"). Immediately the girl stood up and began to
walk around (she was twelve years old). At this they were completely
astonished.*

—Mark 5:35–36, 40–41 NIV

*You're here and I know You are moving
I'm here and I know You will fill me.*

—Brandon Lake, "Rest on Us"

Sunday, February 19

"**A**sbury Revival" peaks in its popularity as a Google search
trend today plus millions of views on TikTok, millions of
Facebook and Instagram views, and hundreds of thousands of new
follows. While I do not know this at the time, what I do know is that
people do not stop coming to worship.

The doors open at 1:00 p.m. for worship and prayer, the altar is open, no spoken invitation needed, just the presence of Jesus beckoning people to come, kneel, and surrender. Hughes fills quickly, as does the lawn outside and the other auditoriums and churches in the area. At 2:00 p.m. the programmed ministry time starts. We write out the order of worship on what we can find. Someone drops off brown paper bags for people to use to pack lunches, and we use them to scribble down the simple plan in Sharpie. Greg invites the congregation into worship, and Esther Jadhav, our Asbury point person on intercultural affairs, prays powerfully and prophetically in the Spirit for the unity of the nations.

I am on one side of Hughes, by the altar, and J.D. Walt is at the other side. Greg and Mark Benjamin listen to young people share their testimonies first and discern which are meant for the congregation. A cohort of about seven teenagers and young adults trail on either side of me and J.D. as the worship music fades away for a time of testifying to God at work. J.D. holds the mic for a young woman, and after she shares her story about freedom from suicidal ideations, he pauses.

"Is there anyone who wants freedom today from messages of suicide, depression, and self-harm?" he asks, scanning the congregation.

Bravely, a few rise.

"There is a spirit of death that wants to claim this generation. If you know someone in your life who needs to be free from a spirit of death, will you stand?"

Many more stand.

"God, today we cancel any hold the spirit of death might have on this generation," J.D. prays. He prays against messages of self-harm, depression, and thoughts of suicidal ideation in the power of the Spirit of God.

I know well how a spirit of death tries to claim Gen Z. Depression and suicidal thoughts batter our own students. The numbers of students seeking help for anxiety at the counseling center has trended up year over year through the past decade, not just on our campus, but across the nation. The congregation contends in prayer with J.D., heads bowed, fervently pleading with the Lord in their own prayer circles, many surrounding the people grouping together and placing their hands on the shoulders and heads of Gen Z members. We balance on the precipice between hope and hell in the spiritual battle over a generation.

The power of God during worship, gentle and fierce, rolls like a wave back and forth across the rows. *Anxiety will not claim this generation! A spirit of death will not own them! Generation Z, get up! You are not dead; you are only sleeping! The Enemy lulls you into a sleep of anxiety and depression, but the Spirit of Jesus calls your name!* "Wake up, sleeper, rise from the dead, and Christ will shine on you!" (Ephesians 5:14 NIV).

As the prayer time releases, a powerful peace settles upon us. The room takes on a lighter atmosphere. The faces turn to God and one another. People hug, cry, hold hands, and lean on one another—the body of Christ healing and loving each other. Jesus has not forgotten His people.

Wake up, sleeper! Jesus woke the dead in scripture; even death was not a match for the healing power of Jesus. Moms and dads in scripture came to Jesus with their children, begging for healing. And we see it now.

Let the little children come to me. The words of Jesus animate before our eyes as parents lead their children to Hughes or the simulcast sites. Kids are everywhere.

A father and two boys from Florida wait in line by the side entrance of Hughes. One of the boys, about ten years old, balances on his crutches, his pant leg pegged up on one side, making his loss of leg obvious. The boy struggles with his crutches, clearly showing balancing on one foot was a new experience for him.

"No need for you to wait out here." Taking note of the boy's wobbly struggle, one of the Asbury team unlocks a side entrance for the boys and their dad into Hughes.

"Oh, that would be great! Thank you so much!" Then the dad turns to his boy. "You are doing great, son." He encourages his son again and again as the boy navigates the crutches with effort. "Keep going. There you go! You got this!"

The family ascends their way up the stairwell, slowly, coming into the auditorium to find a seat. The ushers help them find a seat on the main floor. While the ushers manage lines and get people into seats as efficiently as possible, the holy awe of bringing children to Jesus captivates their attention and mine.

I rest on the steps of the stage, learning against the wall, following the parents with their arms full of kids' backpacks and coats, hands holding onto little ones, and front packs with babies, nestled into sleep with my eyes and heart. Parents want their children to be touched by Jesus—and to be healed. Some moms and dads push reclining stroller-style wheelchairs down the aisles or carry children in arms, kids with oxygen tanks and feeding tubes. From the stage, I am aware of the sober mix of desperation and hope on their faces.

A Portuguese family is on the front row with their three-year-old under a tall stained glass window of Jesus. A tiny girl, she reclines in her stroller, staring up at the ceiling, her eyes fluttering now and then but with no expression on her face. "What's her name?" I ask.

They speak little English, and I do not speak Portuguese. I piece together that the girl's name is Alena, the family lives in Atlanta, and doctors do not know how to help their daughter. I pray with my whole heart for sweet Alena that even if she is not able to communicate verbally, her parents will be reassured that the love of Jesus speaks the language of her soul, immersing her in love and peace.

Several other wheelchairs and strollers border the wall at the front. Each parent drove many hours for this time to be in Hughes and in the presence of Jesus. Our team prays over each one. My own tears fall on the children's hands folded across their bellies and their sometimes-staring eyes. These are sick children with truly desperate parents, each mom or dad longing for the hem of the robe of Jesus to touch their child.

My eyes keep being drawn to these children at the side of the front of the stage. I remember the feeling of desperation myself. At five months old, my daughter Emily developed infantile spasms, a catastrophic form of epilepsy. While we battled the constant seizures (as many as seventy a day) with various medicines, I watched my daughter lose her skills of babbling, rolling over, smiling, and even recognizing me. She lost her personality. For a few months, we did not know if her brain development would return. During that time, I could hardly think or even pray more than a barrage of "Please God, please God." Eventually, through exceptional medical care and life-changing medicine, Emily's seizures did stop, and her brain development reengaged, caught back up, and continued. Jesus healed Emily through the power of medical treatment.

The tears of the moms, dads, and grandparents, pain mingled with hope plainly on their faces, cut me to the heart. The people who prayed for Emily also ministered to me. I remember pastors who prayed at the hospital and dear friends who came to my house and prayed. When they placed hands on Emily and wept for her and asked God to move, it was as if the body of Christ held me. In the same way, now my heart and hands reach for shoulders of moms and dads and the feet of sweet little ones, asking Jesus to heal.

In times of turmoil, people are desperate to know they are in the presence of God and that God remembers them. So, in these days of the outpouring love of God, we pray with desperate people again and again. The altar ministry team lines the altars and wears lanyards marked Prayer Team. Trained by Bud Simon, an intercessor, prayer warrior, and friend of both Seedbed and Asbury, the altar ministers truly serve the body of Christ, meeting them in the deepest prayers of urgency and salvation.

People approach the altar for themselves, but they also come for people they love. When we pray, often the moms and grandmas do not skip a beat naming the loved ones they carry in their hearts. They beg God for their grandkids, their husbands, and their children. They lay on their stomachs and extend their hands to the altar, faces buried in the carpet, shoulders shaking with sobs. I witness the contending prayer of many moms seeking the power of God on behalf of their loved ones. I join them on the floor, laying my hands on their backs as they pour out tears face down and earnestly beg God for a miracle. My prayers echo theirs, seeking freedom from fear, growing faith, and sealing their identity as children of God. People call in prayer requests to our main switchboard. They text us requests, write them on the whiteboard (hundreds of requests!) and pass them to us on slips of paper. Thousands of prayer requests pass through email, many for healing, and our alumni and friends of Asbury, specifically the Titus Women of the Francis Asbury Society, intercede in different parts of the country.

As I pray over one student, a hand rests on my back, and then a warm sensation of the power of God falls on me. I turn around and see an intercessor and faculty member, Sam Kim, leaning over me, and she is praying as I pray. Sam's presence holds Jesus. I wonder at the power of how supporting one another in prayer matters. When we pray for one another, we are the body of Christ, interceding for one another, praying bold prayers for healing and freedom from fear over one another.

Embodied experiences together in worship and prayer matter. People want to show up together, to breathe the same air and sing the same songs, because we need to experience the body of Christ with one another.

Some miracles do happen. A few of our students pray for a man with a tumor in the side of his neck that they see and feel. They pray for over two hours, and the tumor shrinks and disappears under one student's fingers.

An alumna and friend, Sue Gonzalez, has a traumatic brain injury and is not able to manage any loud sounds. "It hurts my brain," she says, describing how a flushing toilet, crackling paper, or hair dryer disturb her—like fingernails on a chalkboard. Noise stresses her brain to the point of causing pain down her neck and a sensation of panic across her body. Sue wears special ear plugs all the time to take the noise level down and help her brain process. She often experiences panic, anger, and anxiety from an overload of sound.

As Sue worships in the balcony as far away from the stage as is possible with her special earplugs in, suddenly the sound turns off. She does not hear anything. Her eyes are closed; she assumes the music has stopped. She takes out her ear plugs and realizes the music continues, but her brain suddenly processes the sound normally, and the sound no longer feels jarring and painful. A wave of peace comes over her, and the presence of God descends upon her from the top of her head, down through her body, and tears of joy trickle down her face. Sue testifies that her brain is reset, and she is able to process sound in a typical way. For the first time in years, Sue worships without ear plugs, kneels at the altar, and prays in the middle of the mash of music, altar prayer, and the buzz of a thousand people all at once.

A retired professor walks in with a blind alumna who has flown in from Colorado. Upon arriving, the Asbury graduate can only see blurs about ten feet ahead of her. After healing intercession, the alumna testifies to her sight increasing to twenty feet, thirty feet, then to forty, fifty, and sixty feet.

More stories of healing emerge—standing and walking a few steps from a wheelchair, the recovery of a sore back, and other relief from pain. People share accounts of healing on social media and to whoever listens.

As the evening unfolds, Zach and I stand at the front after Delvin Pikes, a previous chapel speaker and member of the board of trustees, preaches. Zach's wife, Kristin, and five-year-old daughter, Eden, worship with us. Eden and my daughter Emily share a sweet friendship, and Eden blesses Emily with quick inclusion and love. Emily blesses Eden with a ready playmate always up for a dance party.

The back of the stage overflows with students joyfully jumping in worship. Kristin and Eden join and jump in worship on the stage as well, holding hands with students and spinning in circles, laughing until they cry happy, beautiful tears.

I look over at Zach, and his eyes shine with tears. He wipes them away with the backs of his hands.

"See that?" he says, "I've got my wife back."

I know immediately what he means. After losing their daughter Esther a couple of years before, the pain of loss blanketed Kristin in grief. But tonight, Zach senses the miracle of joy flooding over his wife.

Surely Esther is joining in the singing tonight with Jesus, spinning in circles just like her sister. My heart expands and stretches, taking in the goodness of God and the grief of the world. Jesus did not miraculously heal Zach and Kristin's daughter. Most of the kids with challenging medical situations around the altar tonight will not be healed this side of heaven.

Thirty years ago, as a young adult myself, I served in Kolkata, India, in one of Mother Teresa's homes for handicapped and dying children. I can still see the room in my mind's eyes, The Sisters of Charity, with their white saris and blue ribbons sewn into their head coverings, leaning over little ones who could not feed themselves, washing emaciated limbs, and caring for teenagers the size of toddlers. The presence of Jesus was in that room too, heartbroken with us, with the children, with the sisters. I sensed God there and I sense God here, at Asbury. The broken heart of Jesus breaks with us in this outpouring of love with the hope of heaven and the celebration of the restoration of these little ones around the throne. Jesus said, "Let the little children come to me, and do not hinder them, for the kingdom of heaven belongs to such as these" (Matthew 19:14 NIV).

"Come, Lord Jesus," I ask. "Come, Jesus, in the suffering; come in the grief; come in the loss. I know You hold all things in Your hands." Scripture tells us to lay hands on the sick and pray for them. Our work is to pray; we trust the outcome to the Lord. While we may not understand God's timing, we know that in eternity minds and bodies are whole and free.

The voice of Jesus resonates deeply inside of me, inside of Hughes, the love of God pouring out, running down on all of us—*Don't be afraid, just believe. One day every child will get up through the power of My Name. Talitha koum.*

10

Day and Night

*"Come to me, all you who are weary and burdened,
and I will give you rest.
Take my yoke upon you and learn from me, for I am gentle and humble
in heart, and you will find rest for your souls. For my yoke is easy and my
burden is light."*

—Matthew 11:28–30 NIV

*Worthy is the Lamb, who was slain, to receive power and wealth and
wisdom and strength and honor and glory and praise!*

—Revelation 5:12 NIV

Day and night, night and day, let incense arise!

—David Brymer, "Worthy of It All"

Monday, February 20

Acold winter morning dawns, and the temperature remains freezing at 9:00 a.m. We wonder about the crowds in the line. Slowly the temperature begins to rise but waiting in the cold for hours chills people to the bone. Someone donates heat lamps along the semicircle drive, and our team members purchase all of Wal-Mart throw blankets and pass them out through the line. Families huddle together for warmth and switch out under the heaters.

Early in the morning Joanna Coppedge and her four daughters vacuum and clean Hughes, preparing for a day of worship. An alum and missionary, Jo serves our team from dog walking to washing dishes for people to making food for the volunteers. Jo looks up to see a police officer guiding in a large group of people entering from the side door. Hughes is not yet open to the crowds; however, one of the worship team members plays the piano and another sings quietly at the front through the din of the vacuum cleaner, keeping a constant strand of worship rising to God. This unbroken worship rises from the heart of the worship stewards who want to bless Jesus.

Jo turns off the vacuum and walks over to the officer. "What's going on?"

The officer whispers, "I just had to let them in. They showed up in their van from New Orleans, all eighteen of them in a fifteen-passenger van. They've been driving for nine hours. They have to turn around and go back to work; they can't wait in the line. See, these women, they've been begging to come in and pray."

As he speaks, the group's coats fall to the floor where they stand and their knees drop before the altar. A work crew of some sort—men, and women, none of whom speak much English, but all fully speak the language of the Spirit. Immediately, they lean over the altar, their quiet cries and prayers pour forth instantaneously.

Jo's heart wrenches for the work crew and their desperate need for Jesus, their willingness to come all this way for a few minutes at the altar. Jo and her daughters fervently pray as they clean the auditorium—*Jesus, will You meet the deepest needs of their hearts?*

For half an hour the New Orleans work crew pray with intensity, then leave, cramming back into their van to drive the nine hours back home.

Later, the worship team slips away to pray and rest for a short bit, the piano silent for a rare few minutes. Again, the police officer opens the side door, and a mom, dad, and two children slip in. Before Jo can say anything, the family hurries on the stage and the dad slides onto the piano bench and the girls start to sing.

Jo quickly comes up to the stage. "Friends, no one is supposed to be up here. You may not understand this, no worship team person comes to the stage unless they have been prayed over and consecrated. I am so sorry, but . . ."

The dad stops playing and turns his attention to Jo. "Please, please listen, our family—we've been fasting since the revival started that we might get to play this piano in Hughes and worship." Mom, dad, girls are silent and hopeful, eyes focused on Jo.

Madeline enters at just this moment and discerns to honor the request. The family praises God with five housekeepers, a police officer, the worship steward leader, and Jesus as their congregation. The sweet voices of the family and sound of the piano echo throughout with quiet praise and exaltation, "I exalt Thee. . . . I exalt Thee."

Over the days, Jesus works around our human door-keeping policies to do His work even as we steward the movement. From the police officer who offers compassion to those in the line, to the unauthorized Facebook and YouTube livestream we vigilantly try to shut down and the press we do not invite, the story of the outpouring and the experience of the presence of Jesus will not be ignored. One thing is sure: it is not under human control, ours, or anyone else's.

The cabinet assembles in a glassed-in conference room late Monday morning. We recount the challenges over the weekend of the crowds on the city infrastructure, the ongoing lines in the cold, concerned parents and doubling safety measures around the residence halls. We also name the blessings: many alumni words of encouragement, support of the board, no reports of significant security issues, the hedge of spiritual protection around Asbury, the volunteers, the Asbury team, and the obvious sweet presence of Jesus lingering with us.

We also make the decision to start livestreaming. With our announcement of the last day being Thursday, plus the focus on Gen Z, we hope livestreaming will encourage people to stay home and worship. Obviously, our attempt to discourage streaming from the floor of Hughes has extremely limited success. Unaware of our challenge to stop streaming, my own mom tells me she is watching a bootlegged YouTube version in her living room.

One big question still hovers. Will February 23 be the end of the Asbury ministry, or will the ministry be moved somewhere else in Wilmore? We know we would have to move the services off campus. Our academic mission remains, and we prioritize the care, safety, and support of the 1,100 students on our campus. The idea of moving the outpouring to another location seems implausible. Even if a location might be found, could our Asbury team and the massive group of volunteers we would need to coordinate move with us?

I feel the tension deep in my heart. To stand up under the outpouring of God's love is the honor of a lifetime. Stewarding the movement of God may be the most significant spiritual experience of my life. The flood of people, the desperation to meet Jesus, the joy of worship—all are an undeniable gift of God. Historically, movements of God have led to spiritual awakening in North America, which significantly shaped culture. Is this outpouring part of a spiritual awakening on a national and even an international level? How can we stop stewarding this miraculous work of God, yet how can we continue?

The conversation and discernment burns within all of us.

The outpouring core team carries our lunch trays into the dining room off of the dining hall. I set my plate of roast chicken and salad on the table with a cup of hot lemon tea and honey. My throat feels a little scratchy, and I sip the quickly cooling cup. We pull our dry-erase board over to the table and list the agenda items: afternoon ministry time, evening ministry time, teaching topics, discerning the future of the outpouring.

I scan the faces of these friends of mine, gathered together in a way we never could have imagined. At times, I experience overwhelming emotions as a part of this team. I have never felt more alive in my call as a pastoral leader, yet I physically feel the competing responsibilities in my gut. Asbury students, my role as a university leader, my pastoral call, the people in the lines, Gen Z college students, Asbury teammates, the friends around the table, and my own children at home all threaten to pull my heart into pieces.

As a team we also still struggle for consistent faces of color at the table. Madeline continues to be a strong voice for diversity. Ben and Georges exhort us in the same way with tears. The commitment to multiethnic worship teams is unwavering, and we earnestly want the same for our core group. To steward a movement of God, we need the shared leadership of women, men, diverse ethnicities, multiple ages, and perspectives. I recognize a layer of responsibility to create a diverse group in my dual role of co-convening the group and serving on the president's cabinet. As diversity is important to all of us, and we need all the voices at the table. Shared leadership is not about a "best practice"; it is about the way of Jesus. We press on to call one another to be faithful to this commitment, and the core team develops a multiethnic expression in the next days that persists.

Sometimes, the emotional, physical, and spiritual pressure of scaffolding the movement sweeps through us. Today, one of the group members leans on the table and weeps for some time, shoulders shaking, tears streaming unheeded. The intersection of physical exhaustion with spiritual and emotional weight overwhelmingly converge at times. Some of us are serious and stoic, and others wipe away tears or even sob profusely, kneeling on the floor or even laying down on the floor, head in hands. For me, I acknowledge the tension in my belly, and as the days pass on, I grow quiet and withdraw from the group at times because I do not know how to process the range of emotion I experience. Nevertheless, as we labor together, the Spirit of Jesus guides us gently in the midst of our emotional responses.

I leave the cafeteria, crossing the sidewalks occupied with our students going to class and chatting with friends removed from the lines around the front of campus. What an honor to get to serve students at Asbury at such a time as this. A bit of bleak sun crosses the overcast sky, and I shift my backpack from one shoulder to the other. A scripture passage wafts through my memory: "Take my yoke upon you, and learn from me, for I am gentle and humble in heart, and you will find rest for your souls. For my yoke is easy, and my burden is light" (Matthew 11:29–30).

I wonder at this passage. This outpouring certainly does not seem like a light burden. In a flash, I know in my gut: *But this is not your burden; it belongs to Me to carry.*

On my way back to Hughes, my mind swirling, I walk across campus to the front lawn, covered with people singing and worshipping on the grass and in the line. On a sidewalk on city property adjacent to the campus, a street preacher shouts angry warnings at the crowd in a combative voice, but no one seems to take much notice. Street preachers pop up, sometimes preaching antagonistic messages to the gospel of peace proclaimed in Hughes, obviously out of sync with the outpouring. The crowd just ignores them for the most part.

"I am lowly and gentle in heart," said Jesus (Matthew 11:29 RSV). "*Jesus, I want to learn from you,*" I pray as I breathe. "*Teach me the way of trust, not control.*"

A large group of people gather on the front lawn shouting and aggressively exorcising demons. I text the outpouring core team, "We could use some help on the lawn." Flags unfurl across the green, and shofars blow randomly in line. The outpouring ground team kindly meets each situation. The team does not seek to assess the spirituality or credibility of what is occurring, but instead, with absolute clarity, hold to what we know. God showed up in Hughes in those first forty-eight hours with peaceful worship of singing, confession, repentance, and testimony. With this plumbline, the ground team consistently seeks to stop other spiritual expressions on our campus, not out of any kind of judgment but simply out of obedience to how we initially saw God at work. Almost without exception, people express humility, grace, and kindness when the ushers ask them to put away a shofar, roll up a flag, or pray in a different way to honor the way God worked in those first hours. Nevertheless, wisdom and discernment are required for each of the hospitality team members as they shepherd the guests.

I slip into the warmth of Hughes, but out on the steps, Lisa Harper and Taylor Collingsworth, alumni team members, manage the lines in the chill. Over the last few days, two lines have emerged, one for Gen Z and one for everyone else, with priority seating for Gen Z. Despite the ongoing simulcast and now livestream, people still want to get into Hughes. With the afternoon being the only opportunity for families and individuals above the age of twenty-five, the pressure to get into Hughes increases exponentially.

Hospitality and genuine friendliness are hallmark traits at Asbury. For us, Asbury purple—our main school color—means to put the other person above ourselves. "Being purple" is code for "Demonstrate the Asbury way of authentic kindness." Lisa and Taylor, and the Asbury team, personify purple. Turning people away from Hughes is against our nature, but for the people on the steps, holding back the crowd to prioritize Gen Z is painful.

"Can I just touch the door?" pleads one man.

"Can I just go kneel at the altar for five minutes?" cries some women together.

"Please. I drove so many hours."

A woman who flew from South Korea breaks down and wails, throwing her hands to her face, weeping.

At 4:00 p.m., the final deadline for entry of adults into Hughes is set at 5:00 p.m. that same day. As the minutes tick by, about fifty people wait to be let in. The team determines to ask a core team leader, Mark Benjamin, if he will ask Hughes worshippers to create a space for someone who has not yet been inside. Mark makes the announcement, and many people leave and go to other venues in Wilmore. When the team announces the good news to the remaining people in line, the people whoop and celebrate, dancing on the steps. The team members holding the line cry with relief and gratitude. It means so very much to get everyone in who has waited in line for Hughes that day.

Unfortunately, the announcement goes out across the livestream to the other Wilmore locations—"Space is opening!"—and people literally run to Hughes. *Run.* When Lisa sees them coming, she immediately texts for help from other ushers. At an extreme low point, tempers flare and an usher dodges a guest's fist. It is an emotional day for everyone, and for our Asbury team at the door it threatens to feel defeating.

WhatsApp Thread

[2/20/23, 1:37:45 PM] Glenn Hamilton: How many spaces available at ATS. I'm sending people across the street? I'm working the line.

[2/20/23, 1:40:01 PM] Christine Endicott: We seated 1500 in 30 minutes!!

[2/20/23, 1:40:47 PM] Michelle Kratzer: You are amazing!!!

[2/20/23, 1:41:00 PM] Michelle Kratzer: We need an update on the number of spots on the Seminary side. Can anyone help us with that?

[2/20/23, 1:41:04 PM]

[2/20/23, 1:41:12 PM] Michelle Kratzer: I will send them to you.

[2/20/23, 1:41:14 PM]

[2/20/23, 1:41:33 PM] Maria Brown: Michelle we are sending a prayer person over and they will take some.

[2/20/23, 1:42:33 PM] Michelle Kratzer: Is there someone at the student center at the Seminary who is on this thread, or should I run over and get a count of spaces there?

[2/20/23, 1:43:17 PM] Jessica LaGrone: Hold on one minute.

[2/20/23, 1:43:57 PM] Christine Endicott: I can send tissue to Estes.

[2/20/23, 1:46:16 PM] Michelle Kratzer: Maria did it.

[2/20/23, 1:47:23 PM] Jessica LaGrone: Seminary gym can open at 2:00. Send us people![2/20/23, 1:49:17 PM] Michelle Kratzer: Sending

[2/20/23, 1:49:34 PM] Michelle Kratzer: Is there someone there to receive them and tell them the livestream will start at two?

[2/20/23, 1:49:47 PM] Michelle Kratzer: Also, is the cafeteria full?

[2/20/23, 1:50:18 PM] Jessica LaGrone: We are not currently opening seminary cafeteria. Just our gym until further notice

[2/20/23, 1:52:48 PM] Jessica LaGrone: Holding the line outside Estes until gym opens at 2. Then we'll ask if they'd like to move to open spaces in our gym

[2/20/23, 1:54:56 PM] John Morley: There are three folks in HU107. Students waiting outside to get in Social Work class.

[2/20/23, 1:59:52 PM] John Morley: Nvrmind, We're good.

[2/20/23, 2:04:49 PM] Matt Barnes : Does anyone have any spare tissues? We could probably use half a dozen boxes If not more.

[2/20/23, 2:05:02 PM] Michelle Kratzer: Where?

[2/20/23, 2:05:24 PM] Michelle Kratzer: We'll bring them.

[2/20/23, 2:07:00 PM] Lisa Harper: Can we get another police officer to the Asbury tent? We have one and we probably need two. Thank you.

[2/20/23, 2:08:52 PM] Matt Barnes: Gym for tissues

[2/20/23, 2:09:51 PM] Christine Endicott: Coming with tissues.

> [2/20/23, 2:22:25 PM] Christine Endicott: Gym will likely be full in next 30 min. People pouring in.

> [2/20/23, 2:22:52 PM] Lisa Harper: Wow!!!

> [2/20/23, 2:27:58 PM] Matt Barnes: Gym is going to need at least 4 more prayer people.

> [2/20/23, 2:29:36 PM] Matt Barnes: Never mind. We have lots now.

> [2/20/23, 3:03:04 PM] Michelle Kratzer: Spontaneous, singing all along the line for Hughes. It's pretty beautiful.

In the midst of all this, Michelle Kratzer steps through the Hughes lobby to assist some guests as a hospitality usher. Michelle hears a man loudly weeping in a cement stairway that runs from balcony to basement. Unknown to him, his cries are reverberating through the stairwell and into Hughes. Tears pour freely down the man's face as he is having a deep encounter with the Holy Spirit. Michelle lays her hand on his arm, thanks him for his faith, and invites him to move outside and pray in the stone prayer garden beside Hughes.

At the same time, another man bursts into the stairwell and starts rebuking Michelle. "What are you doing? Why are you making that man stop praying? Who do you think you are? You cannot quench the Spirit!"

With an aggressive and agitated tone, his voice crescendos, and Michelle freezes on the spot, unsure of how to respond to the man thundering through the echoing space. The sobbing man is encountering Jesus—in no way does she want to quench the Spirit—and the shouting of the second man paralyzes her for a moment.

After pausing and whispering a prayer, Michelle turns around to face the man who is raging. "Please do not yell at me," she says firmly. "Could you please, instead, pray for me?"

The man's jaw opens and shuts. Suddenly silent, he looks directly in her eyes and his body changes. His shoulders drop and he becomes quiet and motionless in the stairwell, seemingly praying for her. In the few minutes that pass, it feels as though the Holy Spirit weaves them together—Michelle, the weeping man, the rebuking man—with the threads of a shared hunger for God and a supernatural sensation of the love of God, as angels encircle them with a holy presence.

Another usher slips into the stairwell and gently leads the weeping man into the stone prayer garden beside Hughes and locates an altar minister to pray with him. As Michelle follows them outside into the late afternoon, she contemplates the moment in her heart, pondering it as we do often in these days, the humble and beautiful encounters with strangers and with Jesus. She returns to usher at the back row, listening to the rise and fall of the voices in worship, the Spirit of God blowing peace and grace into every space in the building and every space within our beings. "You are worthy of it all," the people sing. "You are worthy of it all."

I linger on the steps of the stage. Michelle and I are separated across the auditorium by a thousand people, yet very much in the same place in the Spirit. The hearts of the crowd are open to God at the altar. I slide onto the floor, kneel at the altar too, touching the smooth wood with my hands, leaning my forehead against it. I knelt at this same altar as a student when I surrendered my heart to God thirty years before. Worn from tens of thousands of people praying, tears shed, anger poured out, hurt laid bare upon it, the simple wood beams are transformed into a mercy seat. God meets people here. God meets people everywhere, all the time, but God dwells here in this thin place, intersecting heaven and earth. "May [our] prayer[s] be set before you like incense," said the psalmist (Psalms 141:2 NIV). The prayers of God's people cultivate a beautiful fragrance here.

Rob Lim, evangelist and faculty member in the business school, preaches in the evening. Turning to 2 Corinthians 12:9, he proclaims a message on how the full power of God is released in our place of deepest weakness. In a culture in which status, personal power, wealth, and physical strength give the illusion of control, security, and autonomy, it is really in our lack of power, our weakest moment, when the power of Christ takes over and rescues us.

"Imagine if every place with the name Church on its building surrendered to Christ. What would it look like if our spiritual mothers and fathers totally surrendered? What would happen if this generation surrendered to Christ? What will happen?" Rob proclaims prayerfully, heart extended to the congregation.

Jeannie catches the invitation. "The way to the Spirit-filled life is the surrendered life. The way to the abundant life is the crucified life. It's the giving up of everything we are so that Christ may dwell in us. This is a moment of full surrender for some of us in this room. It's a laying down of everything that we are, our past, present, and future. It's a laying down of our hopes, our desires, our appetites, our preferences, our sexuality. . . . It's a laying down of everything that we are so that the Spirit might dwell inside of us. Some of us have known Jesus as our Savior, but this is the moment Jesus becomes our Lord."

The young generation are responding in worship as Jeannie exhorts them to full surrender.

I head home early to help my son, Kai, with a school project, shifting gears in my head as I cross campus. As I come in the door, Emily clings to me; her happy welcome of "Mama 'ome!" is both beautiful and a little bit heartbreaking. At the dining room table, I help my son cut out construction paper for his project and place stickers level across the top of the trifold board. Emily cannot get close enough to me, and she drapes her body against mine, refusing to be moved. I shift her to a more comfortable position on my lap and press my cheek against hers.

"Are you leaving again?" Kai asks as I tuck him into his top bunk that night. I tiptoe on the lower mattress of the T-shaped bunk set and lean over his bed. My hand rests on his heart.

"I don't know," I say truthfully. My energy feels low, like I am a bit sick. "I miss you a lot, Kai. Jesus is doing such big things; I just feel like I need to be in Hughes a lot."

"I know. Kids are asking me about it at school. The teachers want to know about the revival."

"It's a cool thing, huh?" I say, kissing his forehead.

Emily sleeps in the room across the way, piled high with stuffed animals and her favorite blanket. I watch her sleep as parents sometimes do.

Just a few more days, I remind myself.

Siting on the edge of the couch, I start to pull on my shoes to go back over to Hughes. Instead, I lean back against the cushions and pull out my phone. I will rest and check the WhatsApp and the text thread just for a moment.

A ping and a picture pops up that Jeannie sends to the text group:

> I just met Seth who gave his life to Christ here early this week and wanted to mark the work of Jesus! —Jeannie

The picture showed a tattoo of the date 2/16/23 on Seth's hand. I hear Jeannie's voice in my heart: "Let's go!"

> Wow, sealing his commitment! I love it! —Greg
> Keeping this pic! —Kevin

I heart the image and smile, and sitting up with my phone in my hand, I fall fast asleep.

11
Beloved

And the Holy Spirit descended on him in bodily form like a dove.
And a voice came from heaven: "You are my Son, whom I love;
with you I am well pleased."

—Luke 3:22 NIV

All your promises are Yes and Amen.

—Chris Tomlin, "Faithful"

Tuesday, February 21

I have never seen you so tired in our whole marriage." Clint walks with me across campus, slowly, catching me up on the kids and carrying my bag. Never so tired! That is saying a lot. Clint and I have traveled internationally quite a bit over the years, taking college students and our own small children on mission trips together and struggling with jet lag. He also knows the exhaustion from the births of three children, the postpartum transition, and a couple of week-long hospital stays with our youngest.

"Are you sure?" I croak and laugh at myself. The cold settled in my throat, and I sound raspy.

It is an unseasonably warm day, the sun shines with springlike weather, and the lawn surges with worshippers, coats thrown off.

Clint and I chat with a few people in the line, and then I reach the outpouring ground team's logistics meeting.

Members of the ground team take seats at desks dotted around the Morrison building classroom. Glenn Hamilton, both cabinet member and shepherd, joins the group and holds deep compassion for the crowds and his team, including the maintenance crew, managing custodial support, financial issues, and crisis repairs with constant care. Paul Stephens facilitates the conversation. Over the weekend a volunteer flew into Lexington from Phoenix to assist us with the overall event management. A donor paid for the event manager, an expert and professional of massive conference management, to come, and she fits into the ground team seamlessly and quickly becomes irreplaceable—another outpouring miracle.

I notice the open laptops, the focused faces, and the unending commitment to Jesus and Asbury in the members' words and actions. Each member of the ground team demonstrates not only incredible logistical skills but hearts for ministry for the Asbury departments they represent and for genuine care for people in the lines.

Over the days volunteers showed up miraculously for the most part; but today we need more volunteers, and we also need more prayer ministers. I send out an SOS to Jessica Avery for altar ministry and to our core team to call in any reinforcements they know of from local churches.

The ground team works through issues, problem solving, and debating how to handle various logistical challenges. The team asks about the plan for after February 23. Where is the outpouring going? It remains the topic of the day.

In the afternoon, I cross the street to Asbury Theological Seminary, praying for wisdom as I go. I dodge groups of people, step past the lines for free food and coffee and row of portable toilets. We have a meeting scheduled to discuss the future of the outpouring.

People mill around the front of Estes Chapel on the seminary side of the street. In the early afternoon, light rain washes the sidewalks, and a few people gather under umbrellas and don rain jackets. I wear my Kelly green rain jacket, and thankfully the rain holds off from drenching me.

To my astonishment, all three of the Free Methodist bishops are together in front of Estes Chapel. Ordained as a Free Methodist, I immediately sense encouragement at seeing the church elders. The bishops place their hands on me and pray earnestly for wisdom, strength, and perseverance. My heart lightens.

"I am preaching tonight," I mention with a smile. "Please pray for me." The bishops ask God for the grace and goodness of God to fall upon my head.

I duck into the seminary administration building late and join a meeting already in progress with Timothy Tennent, president of Asbury Theological Seminary, about the future of the outpouring. David Thomas, J.D. Walt, and Kevin Brown also have seats around the table. The window blinds are open, and across the street the crowds mill and wait. I find my seat and catch up on the conversation.

As we discuss what God is doing through the outpouring and what it means to steward it, I take note of the experience. As we talk, I reflect: *I want to remember this moment always, in the holiness of God's presence and the humanity of pressure as we struggle to discern what we each heard God saying.* I know the privilege to discern together how to steward the outpouring is an honor beyond what I can name. We debate different perspectives with sincerity and emotion around the table, but one shared belief emerges: what God is doing at Asbury is not meant for Asbury only, but for the world. God lit the wick with Gen Z, but the rest of us put our candles in the flame and the fire burns on.

We do not wish to end what we did not start. This belongs to God, and to get to stand up under the outpouring of God's love whether for six hours or sixteen days amazes and humbles us.

As we discern together, we get clear that after February 23 there will be no ongoing services at Asbury or Wilmore, but believe God will not stop pouring out love upon His people

The whole water table of faith is raised across the nation.

Let it be to us according to Your Word.

Kevin reminds us, "A fire is brightest when it is tallest, but hottest when it smolders." The spiritual bonfire flames brightly around the globe these days, but the fire is only growing in intensity as it smolders, ready to flame and spark as the Spirit moves.

In the evening Hughes hosts row after row of students. Jeannie welcomes everyone; Greg gives the call to worship; two students testify; and the congregation worships. I wait at the side to preach, taking in their faces, their energy, their eyes for God. I sense the Holy Spirit rest on my head and a deep impression of the words *You are My beloved daughter.* I remember Jesus rising out of the Jordan river and the Holy Spirit descending upon him with the words, *This is My beloved Son. With You I am well pleased.* In John 15:9, Jesus invites us into this love relationship between the Father and the Son.

"As the Father has loved me, so have I loved you. Now remain in my love" (NIV). The invitation to abide in the love of Jesus summed up the goods new to me. All of us for all of Jesus, the love exchange of a lifetime. All the freedom, all the grace, all goodness upon us. The end of striving, earning worth, and the beginning of abiding and claiming love.

As I preach, my voice cracks and rasps, hoarse from congestion and overuse.

> "Your place of deepest humiliation and shame is the place where Jesus claims you. Jesus died for you not in your grandest moment, but in your worst moment. Not at the top of your game or mine,

but when I am all done in, when I am worn out. That's the moment when Jesus comes in. When you experience the love and freedom of Jesus, you know that you want to put everything out on the altar. Jesus laid his whole life out for you, died on the cross for you. The kingdom of God is this: all of Jesus for all of you. Where is the Holy Spirit working in your spirit this evening?

"I know some of you may be really tired of holding it all together. You don't have to carry that. It does not have to be the story of your life. Or the story of my life. You don't have to live under the bondage of sin and shame and deal with it all your days. The power of Christ is released for you and for me in our sin and our shame. You don't have to live through life with shame upon your shoulders. Jesus came to take your shame!

"If you haven't experienced Jesus before, we want to introduce you to Jesus," I close, my voice fracturing with emotion and exhaustion.

The altar fills again and again, as it does every hour these days. The altar ministry team sits on chairs at one side of the altar with boxes of tissues and Bibles to hand out. The harvest is more than plentiful. We run out of anointing oil, but thankfully, the doorkeepers ate Italian food for dinner, including a large cup of olive oil meant for dipping bread. After prayer over the olive oil, little cups of oil from the restaurant dot the very front of the stage, ready for use for makeshift but still holy anointing. Another sweet outpouring moment.

The bishops who prayed over me earlier join upstairs in the balcony, in the few remaining seats after students had settled into rows. I catch their eyes from the stage, see their hands open in worship and prayer, and sense their joy. What a night to treasure.

At 11:32 p.m. Zach texts:

Grateful for y'all! Can you believe what He has, is and will do?

We all feel the same.

February 22

The core team gathers at 4:30 p.m. to plan the Wednesday evening ministry time, pray, prepare, and linger together. I look around at our team one last time as we discern together how to proceed that evening in worship. These faces have grown very dear to me over the past two weeks. We laugh at jokes about revival-bonding as we pull out the dry-erase board yet one more time.

As a team, over the course of the outpouring we grew stronger and more diverse in ethnicity, especially in the last few days, honoring our partnership of men and women and our commitment to a multiethnic experience on every level. As we reflect on the days of ministry, several themes emerge from our shared experience of stewardship. Our team grew in the soil of shared leadership, mutual discernment, radical humility, step-by-step obedience, and surrender of self to God. The heart of the outpouring is a heart consecrated and surrendered in obedience to Jesus. We encountered the serious invitation of God to go "further up and further in" as C. S. Lewis would say.[1] We experienced worship on campus and at the other sites that was holy and transformative, and the fruit of it is radical consecration of the human soul. The accelerated spiritual growth and change in these days shaped each of the core team beyond words.

The next day, the February 23 service will conclude the outpouring worship in Hughes while integrating the Collegiate Day of Prayer team with the core team. Greg and David carefully work with the CDOP team to cast a vision for the service that will reflect the "no famous Christians," Gen Z–focused, low-production way of the outpouring. Wednesday night will be our last service to steward as a team.

Dan Wilt texts our group, sharing his words about the movement of invitation to benediction of these days:

1. C.S. Lewis, *The Last Battle* (New York: McMillan, 1956), 180.

"Come and see" is [becoming] "go and be"—the love of
God for the world!

Wednesday night, February 22, is a night of commissioning. Go
and be! What's happening in Hughes is not meant to stay here. It's
for the world! News of universities around the country reporting
all-night prayer meetings, baptisms, and unplanned worship nights
continue to spring up. The fire has already jumped from Hughes
Auditorium. Tonight, we commission and bless Gen Z to release the
fire to the world.

Remembering Ash Wednesday, Greg opens the service with
Psalm 51 and invites the congregation into a posture of repentance
on their knees. The worship team kneels on the stage, nose to carpet,
the ancient and true words echoing across the people.

> Create in me a pure heart, O God,
> and renew a steadfast spirit within me.
> Do not cast me from your presence
> or take your Holy Spirit from me.
> Restore to me the joy of your salvation
> and grant me a willing spirit, to sustain me. (vv. 10–12 NIV)

Students give testimonies, Mark and J.D. shepherd the students
to read their life scriptures, Zach preaches, and Jeannie catches the
invitation to surrender to Jesus. The whole team feels the significance
of this last evening of the core team stewarding ministry with Gen Z,
the blessing of it all, and the fellowship in the Spirit.

"How Great Is Our God,"[2] rings through Hughes.

The beauty of the voices carries praise to heaven.

At some point in the evening, I head home, physically spent
with the cold held at bay finally catching up with me. I sleep for
hours, but the next day I still stay on the couch, my body aching. My
kids arrive home from school and squeeze with me on the couch, not

---

2. Chris Tomlin, Jesse Reeves, and Ed Cash, "How Great Is Our God," track 3 on Chris
Tomlin, *Arriving, Sparrow/sixstep, 2004, studio album.*

minding my sneezes and coughs. Simply being together feels good. One kind friend drops off chicken noodle soup, and others bring gifts of brownies, muffins, and a Mexican casserole. We eat, snuggle under heaped blankets on the couch, and pray the hours together through the joy of simply being present.

After I tuck the kids in for the night, I watch the Collegiate Day of Prayer service from my bed under a comforter. An estimated 3 million people worship and pray for awakening on campuses from across the planet. With diverse faces across the stage and young adults sharing Jesus alongside the over-fifties, the Holy Spirit pours forth through their hearts on the livestream. Students worship on the stage and in the auditorium, exuding another taste of heaven on earth. A room of Gen Z—our students as well as students from other campuses and high schools—occupy the seats.

Kevin welcomes the worshippers in the auditorium and from around the world.

"I just want to say this was not planned. This was not a function of an innovative, state-of-the-art facility. It was not a function of a slick marketing scheme. There was no program planning committee. And it's not because of celebrities or professional musicians. This has been a nameless, title-less movement, and tonight will be no different".

The congregation applauds with joy. From inside of Hughes to outside on the semicircle lawn to across the street at Estes Chapel and the other locations throughout these sixteen days, Jesus Christ is the center of attention. As Kevin shares that evening, this movement of God demonstrated what we know of God from James 3:17—it was pure, peaceable, gentle, yielding, full of mercy, and full of fruit. Days marked by radical humility, compassion, and consecration for thousands, with extravagant hospitality from a team of people made of Asbury, Seedbed, Asbury Seminary, and the people of Wilmore and beyond.

Kevin concludes, "We are seeing this spiritual fire beginning to flare in a variety of other spaces, . . . The trajectory of renewal is always deeper. The trajectory of renewal is always outward. [This is] the missional instinct to bend the universe in favor of our neighbor, in favor of the widow, in favor of the orphan, in favor of the alien—the compulsion to bear witness to a different king and to a different kingdom with the political statement that 'Jesus is Lord.'"

The evening service unfolds with student testimonies, an invitation to know Jesus, and calls to pray for an awakening across the globe for college students and others. Even though the last two weeks resonate with words of witness and worship, the music and students feel fresh and inhabit the wind of the Spirit.

Layers of emotions cover me like the blankets. A blanket of real joy settles on me as Gen Z worships over the livestream. A layer of God's warm love rests on me. But then, a blanket of disappointment falls over me as well. After these days of being present in Hughes, not being in the room during this final service is sad. I remember the Asbury team who spent most of these days managing the lines, organizing trash runs, doing the tech for the livestream or simulcast, and serving as ushers at the door. In or out of Hughes, the presence of Jesus breathed on us. A few more tears well in my eyes as the emotions and gratitude compound. What a gift we stewarded, and the holiness and awe continue now in us. I slowly close my laptop even as I reach for a tissue. My body aches and my nose runs, but deep within my soul, I taste the oil of joy and the vinegar of grief, shaken together as the sixteenth day closes.

At 10:37 p.m., with the livestream signing off, Kevin types on the WhatsApp thread:

Well done, everyone! Well done.

The words of celebration and gratitude to one another abound on our phones. The musicians pack up their instruments, and the IT team turns off microphones and close down the livestream. Almost 380 hours conclude, the spontaneous act of God released to the world.

WhatsApp Thread

[2/24/23, 10:24:10 AM] Kevin Brown: You all are the best.

[2/24/23, 10:26:03 AM] Maria Brown: You deserve more thanks than you will ever get. So amazed by all the work and service and your joyful spirits.

[2/24/23, 10:28:08 AM] Mark Troyer: So blessed by all [on the WhatsApp thread]. Thanks for your hearts, patience, tenacity and "being holy" in your actions!

[2/24/23, 10:28:39 AM] Barb Boyle: Amen and amen! Thank you all for stepping away from your day jobs to minister to the thousands!!! May you catch up on rest soon!!

[2/24/23, 10:41:56 AM] Michelle Kratzer: What an amazing privilege it has been to serve alongside each of you as we have watched God move. Wow. Just wow. And thank you!

12:24 a.m.

This has been the most unimaginable blessing to serve alongside you. Love to all of you with some rest and peace. —Jessica Avery

"His master replied, 'Well done, good and faithful servant! You have been faithful with a few things; I will put you in charge of many things. Come and share your master's happiness!'"

—Matthew 25:14 NIV

February 25

Saturday morning, I pour my coffee and open laptop and with the kids still asleep, I curl up on the couch. I start to journal, bullet-style, reflecting on some of the moments of the last few days. What do I not want to forget? I jot it down, the words flowing out of my fingers faster than I can think. It makes sense to post it on Facebook, my second and last post of the outpouring.

Day 18: We are returning to ordinary life—which is just as full of God as the last 17 days—just a bit more quiet. I am sure we have a lifetime of journaling, prayer, and deep conversation ahead. Throughout the days as we passed each other in the halls and outside, we kept saying to each other— can you believe this?", "is this really happening?". As theologians and well, everyone, everywhere—name and debate what it was and wasn't, what I do know for sure is that people are longing for God.

- I don't want to forget the Latino family—grandpa, dad, uncle, kids, mama—who when they made it into Hughes after what must have been a wait of hours—didn't even go to their seats. They went immediately to the altar and collapsed in front of it. We saw this again and again.

- I want to remember the family who drove 30 hours each way from Mexico for someone to pray over their baby for healing.

- My heart is broken with the 18 men who piled into a 15 person-passenger van for 9 hours, to pray at an altar for even 30 minutes.

- Holding in my heart the time of prayer with an Indian Pastor and his wife, Diana, from the United Kingdom, interceding for their country and their campuses.

- Who can forget the Brazilians! They showed up! Their passionate prayers for their country! All the Brazilian flags (although graciously put away when we asked—just too many people for all the flags!).

- The story of a police officer who was so moved that he got in a family (with two younger kids) who had been fasting through the lines and waits out of his sheer compassion.

- As a mom of a daughter with special needs, the families who brought their children for prayer for medical issues, just broke my heart. Their faith, their desperation, I feel it with them. I will continue to pray for Alena.

- Trying to communicate thru an app with a couple in Portuguese. Making a mental note: next time, we need to be prepared for interpreters! (kidding, kidding about the next time!).

- Remembering the pastor couple from Chile who sold their car to be here. And strangers passing on money—"Can you give it to the lady who sold the car?" YES!

- I want to remember people giving what they had—we had no donation box set up—so they handed it to us—"thank you, thank you" people said, "This is what I have to give" whether it was a nickel or a hundred dollars.

- So many high schoolers praying for relief from the bondage of pornography. Parents, step in! Take away phones, keep them out of bedrooms. Your children are DESPERATE.

- A joyful group from a church in San Diego—so full of JOY of being here, thank you for your encouragement!

- Praying with a team from Canada who were full of stories of God on the move in Canada and how God moved on their drive down!

- I want to remember the WhatsApp thread, 101 notifications at a time— "Water needed in Estes!" "Is there a prayer volunteer for out in the line?"; "Portapotties overflowing!"; "10 people gave their hearts to Jesus here!"; "The huge JESUS flag needs to come down!"; "What's that ambulance for?"; "It's 30 degrees out here. Heaters are on the way"; "The Sal Army showed up. Thank you, Jesus!"

Mostly, I will remember our relationships between one another on the ground team, the volunteer team, and the ministry team.

Revival runs on the track of relationships.

As one of our retired professors said, "We were surprised, but not unprepared." We are a small community who loves Jesus deeply.

We weren't ready, but yet we were. God is like that.

We were surprised but not unprepared. God is like that.

12

Benediction

The light shines in the darkness, and the darkness has not overcome it.

—John 1:5

He will turn the hearts of the parents to their children,
and the hearts of the children to their parents.

—Malachi 4:6

May His favor be upon you
And a thousand generations

—Cody Carnes and Kari Jobe, "The Blessing"

Late Spring 2023

Hughes Auditorium, still and quiet, shines in beauty, with sunlight filtering in through the stained glass, the sturdy and worn altar a constant reminder of the call to surrender to Jesus. The words *HOLINESS UNTO THE LORD* in large gold letters govern the room and direct us to God.

As I enter the doors from the side of the stage, a flash of memory comes to me. Often as I trekked back and forth between the volunteer hub and the ongoing meetings, I'd pause before I opened these doors and entered Hughes. I knew when I stepped through the doors, it would be as if I'd jumped into a pool, immersed physically in the love and presence of Jesus. The spiritual sensation of entering Hughes made me want to hold my breath as I plunged through the doors, the presence of God closing over my head.

Now, as I linger in the quiet, the rows of seats, tall windows, and overlooking balconies silently breathe in the Spirit, a gentle exchange of the breath of holiness and ordinary time hovering like an invisible cloud.

Thousands of knees kneeling at the altar, surrendered to Jesus, over the past century marked this place. When the Israelites repented and turned back to the Lord, Samuel took a stone and set it on their path, calling it an Ebenezer, saying "Thus far the Lord has helped us" (1 Samuel 7:12). If the eyes of my heart could see the spiritual world, would I see thousands upon thousands of Ebenezer stones in Hughes? With a holy imagination, the stones cover the altar, and the floors, and then the Ebenezer stones becoming themselves an altar reaching up to the roof and stacking to touch the words *HOLINESS UNTO THE LORD*. Much spiritual work happens here. God moves everywhere; no place is without God, yet when the people of God gather and call on His name together, the power of God meets us in a different way. The Ebenezers of the decades before scaffold the work of God today.

God poured out His love upon His people in those sixteen days of outpouring. From the first day to the release to the world, it was only about Jesus. People came to experience Jesus; I came to experience Jesus. I needed those days.

My own heart beats with a new energy of belief. Seeing firsthand the hunger and expectancy of the crowds awakens in me a fresh faith in God. Experiencing the transforming love of Jesus in our students renews me and reinvigorates my own ongoing journey of transformation.

The days now fill with administrative meetings, student concerns, planning for next year's activities and student leader selection.

Instead of discerning ministry for fifty thousand guests, I meet with the Student Life executive leadership team about budgets and organize the end-of-the-year celebrations. Faculty and students alike stretch their abilities to finish the semester. After the sixteen days of the outpouring, our campus energies are spent. At the same time, many students exude joy in the Holy Spirit, sharing their testimony of death to life in Jesus. Student Life team members and faculty listen to students debrief and hear the witness of what Jesus has done in their hearts over these days.

A flood of invitations for students to testify come from all corners of the United States and the world. God continues to stir the waters around the world for Gen Z. Hardly a day goes by that I do not receive a text about an all-night prayer meeting, a twenty-four-hour church service, multiple college student baptisms from a nation in the world that in some way connects to the outpouring. As much as the spontaneous movement of God in Wilmore surprised me, it surprises me again to see the outpouring at Asbury as a beginning of the work of God in the world in these days to stir up the church, starting mostly with teenagers and young adults.

Guests continues to arrive, watching social media and unaware the services ended. Guests come from the Netherlands, South Korea, Mexico, and all over the United States, expecting to join the ongoing outpouring services and instead join our regularly scheduled chapel services or pray in a mostly empty Hughes.

Now, as I stand quietly by the side of the stage where I'd spent so many hours, a few guests join me in Hughes, slipping to the altar or wandering through the seats. One of the Asbury guest hospitality team hosts them, sharing the story of the magnificent way God showed up. I watch the guests for a time, remembering how I stood on the stage and wonder with awe at the expectant hearts from around the world, worshipping.

My phone vibrates in my pocket, and I ignore it. The prayer of my soul breathes in and out in rhythm with the Spirit, resetting my soul:

> *God, You came! You came for the broken and the tired, for the dead-hearted, and the ones addicted to drugs, pornography, and perfectionism. You showed up for the ones who never went to church and those who were hurt by church leaders. You moved for the ones who carried abuse in their stories, who doubted, who wondered if You are real, those who identified themselves by depression and anxiety.*
>
> *You came for our world and for our nation, for the old people and the poor people, for the ones wealthy in the eyes of the world and the ones all used up and with nothing left to give.*
>
> *Lord, You showed up not just for these generations present, but for their children and their grandchildren. In their family stories, they will share a holy imagination for how You can and will move.*
>
> *In an age where social influencers have access on our devices to shape our souls, God got all our attention, using the very means of the day to give an eyewitness account to Your people at worship.*
>
> *In a world with so much darkness and violence, why, God, would You show up and move in this way? Surely, You were needed much more desperately in other locations and nations.*

I hear the Lord deep in my heart: *When the world becomes darker, My light shines even more brightly.* I pray:

> *Jesus, use these days of the outpouring of Your love to be a light to the nations in these days of growing darkness. You will overcome the world. Your promise to us is Immanuel, God-with-us. In the deepest darkness, the most human suffering, the valley of the shadow of death and our fears and brokenness, You are with us. You are a God who suffers with us, a shining light in dark days.*

My heart burns with the good news of God. My spiritual call never felt more alive than during those sixteen days. *God, I pray, what do you have for me now?* Am I supposed to leave Asbury and serve as a pastor? Do I lean into being a spiritual mother to Gen Z right here at Asbury, in my same office and my same role?

My phone buzzes again and again. I walk out of Hughes and into the bright April sunshine. Even in its exhaustion, the campus bustles with life. Students study on the deck of the student center, play spike ball on the green, are engrossed in energetic conversations as they pass me; others look overwhelmed with the impeding exams. *Buzz.* I hurry through the arches, headed to my next meeting.

Walk more slowly.

Walk more slowly? I slow down—a bit. *God, what do You mean? This is what I ask of you in these days: Walk more slowly.*

I slow down even more, students passing me on either side, almost bumping into me. I look into their eyes. I put my phone away. I pray for them as I pass them. The Lord is so very practical. I am learning that the way of God is simple.

Keep alert for how God is moving. Take note of His pace. Look in your path for who God brings. Be expectant that what God has done, God will do again.

Walk more slowly. Let it be to me according to Your word. I don't want to miss the moment.

My friend, colleague, and core ministry team partner, Jeannie Banter, tells the story of how, while sick with COVID on Feb. 8, she was watching chapel online from her couch, and Liz Louden texted her at 10:24 a.m. before the message even started.

> I don't know if the students know, but the Spirit is here. We just had the most spirit-filled worship.

We believe that when the Holy Spirit began moving in Hughes in such a powerful way, it was the answer to thousands of prayers over decades, asking for God to come and move yet again. For a divine reason, *kairos* and *chronos* time intersected on February 8, and at just the right time (see 2 Corinthians 6:2 NLT), God moved. Students were praying at Asbury for revival and for God to move.

While I do not seek to find a "cause" for why God poured out love on this particular day and at that specific time, I wonder with awe about how God prepared the way. Kevin Brown often quotes a faculty member saying, "Asbury is like a dry riverbed. When the rains come, the water knows where to go." Certainly, over decades and even in the 2022–2023 academic year, God prepared the riverbed for the waters of God to overflow upon us.

One thing is for sure: God sends revival not because things are right, but to set things right.

On February 8, God poured forth love through the Asbury Gospel Choir as a powerful conduit of the Holy Spirit. But their story didn't start there.

February 7, 2023, the Day Before

A few administrators and faculty meet in the board room on the top floor of Kinlaw Library to craft nine principles as an ethos statement to guide our community. I open my laptop and review the document we worked on over the past months. Based on our promise to students to create an environment in which to Belong, Become, and Be Set Apart, are mined from previous statements, we hope to connect the nine principles clearly to how we live together as a community.

We hammer out work on the nine principles, making note of how we live into our ethos and what we aspire to.

I reread some of the principles: "We both affirm and practice a vibrant and earnest commitment to Jesus Christ as Lord and Savior with the Bible as the ultimate authority for our life. We believe that all persons are made in the Image of God and, thus, have inestimable human worth and equal human dignity. "

"How does this inform how we train our students during orientation?" someone wonders.

Toward the end of forming our minds, hearts, and hands—we believe that Christian education is for the body as well as the mind and, therefore, shapes our judgments, sensibilities, and practices for living well. We debate how these practices of living well apply to keeping the Sabbath as an academic community in a way that offers life and blessing. Does having a commitment to Sabbath mean we think differently about exams and projects due on Monday?

These conversations inspire me. The whole ethos team is energized by collaborative work on not just who we are as Asburians, but how we are—how we live and practice our commitments to belonging, becoming, and being set apart.

After the meeting, I pack my tote bag and hurry to the HIC-CUP, the student coffee shop, for an afternoon caffeine refresh. I check my calendar on my phone, mentally go over my constant list of things to do. Next thing: 3:00 p.m. Witnessing Circle.

A few minutes later, I join others in the large multipurpose Luce Auditorium in the Collaborative Learning Center. The tall stained-glass window of an Asbury purple cross heralds the front of the space.

As one of the Black History Month events, a Lexington, Kentucky, pastor and a few friends of Asbury from the region share a witnessing circle as a practice of revisiting place-based tragedies to bear witness to and humanize the victims. While we always celebrate Black History Month on campus, this is the first time we experience a witnessing circle on campus as a way of lament. The wills of mid-1800s Lexington-area property owners archive the passage of slaves—men, women, boys, girls, and infants—to other family members in lists alongside featherbeds, horses, and washstands.

Members of the Asbury community take turns reading the wills. The grief of humans passed on as possessions down the family line sobers all of us, many respond with tears. As the archival records conclude for this witnessing circle, a Haitian American man I don't recognize, Georges Dumaine, steps forward to sing the Black national anthem.

"God of our weary years . . . God of our silent tears . . ." Georges' resonant voice draws us into the words powerfully. As he sings, the people respond not only in song but with emotion. Tears pour down Georges face freely, and something shifts in the room—it is no longer a sober community meeting but a sacred space.

The service concludes but a sense of the sacred stays, and no one moves for a time. Georges weeps, feeling the presence of Jesus surround him in such a profound way he can barely stand. The presence of Jesus abides in the grief, lament, and confession, taking up residence in the remembrance of suffering. People disperse, but the holy moment of the witnessing circle lingers with all of us.

Georges joins Ben and the rest of the Gospel Choir in the evening to rehearse for leading worship on Wednesday, February 8. Zach will be the preacher, and the Gospel Choir will lead three songs along with Ben, the director, and Georges, as a guest and friend. Their preparation turns to prayer, and the Gospel Choir turns their hearts to God, responding to the presence of Jesus that Georges still carries with him. Late into the night, the students pray over the rows of the seats of Hughes, prayers reaching from the stage through the whole space. The strains of worship music drift quietly across the auditorium, a prayer as well. A sweet presence of Jesus wraps around the choir, exuding love and joy but with an urgency for God to move. The collective prayer of the students and others, a yearning for God, dances across Hughes. *Come, Lord Jesus.*

Benediction

In the early morning hours of February 8, the last few members of the Gospel Choir finish their rehearsal and prayer time, gather up their backpacks and music, and return home.

"See you in a few hours for chapel. Good night!"

The old wooden doors close behind them, and they step out into the cold February night. The Spirit of Jesus remains, abiding.

Ready? Let's go!

Afterword

Sarah Thomas Baldwin

One Year Later

One of the most frequent questions I am asked is, "So, did anything change?" In early winter, after all the leaves have fallen in Kentucky, a few of the core team gather in a conference room in the Radar Student Center, overlooking the corridor of sidewalk packed with students on their way to class. Around the room I note faces of color, men and women, across the generations. Over the past months, our core team has met several times, continuing to pray and steward the outpouring of God's love, which is not ceasing but instead ripples out, far-reaching. We keep asking each other: What are you seeing? What are you experiencing? How is God moving now?

I place my coffee mug precariously beside me on the sofa and balance a notebook on my lap. *What are we experiencing at Asbury post-outpouring?* My pen cannot keep up with the flood of thanksgiving:

We are experiencing a reset in Jesus across the campus.

The goodness of God is taking us deeper into Him!

Testimonies of freedom continue!

The campus feels lighter.

The outpouring is a signpost of hope we keep referencing.

The fruit is abundant in our students! Calls to missions.

Calls to social action!

It's like we are "holy marionettes"! God picks us up and is moving us in new life.

We have gone from flat to three-dimensional!

Surrender marks us.

We are sober about the seriousness of the call to steward the outpouring that continues with our students.

This is a light in the darkness!

We are experiencing revival!

Truly, we are experiencing revival. Students linger after chapel to worship and pray frequently. This is just how we are now. Spontaneous times of worship outside on the lawn, students coming together to pray, new commitments to Jesus and baptisms are a part of the life of our community. We are struck with amazement by students who have shown no interest in Jesus—even after last February—who now ask in the manner of the Ethiopian eunuch in Acts 8, "Will someone explain to me the way of Christ?" We see students who want purpose, who desire discipleship, who want to know what is this faith that calls us to "come and die" to self.

Our students have traveled on over fifty-five witness teams in the past months not only in the United States but in other countries as well. The students take the lead in testifying and sharing how God is at work in their lives. Many of our faculty and staff have shared in their churches, small groups, and some even in other countries. It is true to say our spiritual temperature is raised.

It is also true that our students continue to battle anxiety and depression. Our campus is not immune to the deep emotional struggles, loneliness, stress, and physical health concerns that accompany young adults in the college years. Yet, a renewed call to prayer, fresh faith, and revived surrender abides with us.

As I walk through the student center on the way back to my office, I see students pouring over textbooks with coffee and others immersed in conversation with faculty members or hanging out on couches with friends. Everywhere is life and community, people working out together what it means to belong, to become, and to be set apart in God. The spiritual life of a college student is so very practical: genuine relationship and shared life whether it is on an athletic field or in the dining hall, the development of the intellect to know more of God and to think well and deeply, learning what it means to follow Jesus in the beauty of life and when it is raw and painful. This community is part of my formation every day as well, and I am shaped by it.

Reaching my office, I close the door for a moment behind me, pausing in the space a bit to remember what happened for me in those days. I lean across my little table in my office, outpouring cards, art. and even a couple books on the spontaneous move of God around me. Visually, my life is different. The outpouring of God's love has not stopped.

I am different. My spiritual temperature is raised. My sense of calling is deeper; my urgency to the gospel is quicker. The Gospels came to life before my eyes, and I got a front row seat. How could I not be changed?

I still feel overly busy and inundated with tasks at times (okay, often!), but my identity in Jesus is rooted even more deep into the soil of my soul. At times before, I worried that the branches of my life may hit the ceiling and walls of Wilmore and feel confined. Now I hope and pray to be a tree, as in Psalm 1, planted near streams of living water, to bear fruit in season and to be a shelter for others, for these students, for whoever God brings into my path.

What God has done; God will do again. I want to be ready.

Amen.

Asbury University
Early Winter 2024

Afterword

David Thomas

Recently I had the opportunity to meet Heather Holdsworth, the daughter of *Sounds from Heaven* authors Colin and Mary Peckham, who penned the best account of the Hebridean Revival of 1949–52. Mary was a college student at the time of this revival in the islands of far northwest Scotland, what some historians consider to have been the last real spiritual awakening in the Western world. Mary was converted early on in those months and ended up staying in her native Lewis and Harris to serve in the revival throughout its duration.

Heather told me that Mary essentially gave the rest of her life to the retelling of that story. She never tired of answering questions about what it was like in that time to live under an open heaven. From her college years on, Mary's life was marked by an experience that had ruined her for anything less than *the real*—to have been in a room where Jesus is fully present and working.

To some extent, this has been the experience of all of us who laid eyes on the Asbury Outpouring. We are wrecked now, unable to settle for anything less than Christianity in the presence of the Lord. We *had been hopeful* for a better day from reading Scripture and revival history. But now we have a *concrete hope* because it has become our sight. We have a sure confidence that Jesus wants to come and rescue this generation.

And we pray that these emerging adults who witnessed the outpouring, both on Asbury's campus and beyond, will never be able to cut a deal with cultural Christianity from this point on. They have tasted and seen the compelling contrast between "community under outpouring" and the nominal, inert American religion that they have been offered for far too long.

Community under outpouring was what we set out to be and do day-after-day in February of 2023. Having come to believe that we were experiencing a historic outpouring of Jesus' presence, we were attempting each day to build and hold community under it. That actually is not too bad of an understanding of what Pentecost was. "Community under outpouring" is not too far from what Church is, or at least what we long for it to be. Like Mary Peckham, being in a community like that deposited something in us that we will always be eager to pass along to others.

In that retelling, we are not attempting to enshrine the outpouring, not trying to monumentalize it or make something of it that it is not. We look forward to a day soon when there will be another outpouring story that will eclipse this one at Asbury. I hope that story will come from where you are—your city, your campus, your church and family, your own life. We desperately need hundreds of outpourings all over the world for decades. But as long as Jesus can gain any benefit from this story, and there is any measure of curiosity about it, we will continue to recount it.

I am deeply grateful to my friend, Sarah, for this wonderful rendering, and for her invitation to offer a few reflections here at the close. Sarah and I co-facilitated the team that fell into a lifeboat that Wednesday afternoon, February 8, naïve to the fact that we would not get out of that little raft for the next sixteen days! From the vantage point of the shore now, we can see more of what God was doing and is continuing to do from our encounter with Him, first among the young.

Empowering the Young

Every day, to the thousands that kept coming, we would say that "had it not been for a few students lingering that Wednesday morning, none of us would be here. They were the forerunners of this Outpouring, and we are following their lead." Early on we began to observe the favor of God upon the worship, altar, and youth. The middle-aged and elders among us began to see that the more we stepped back and let the youth lead, the more God was working.

Here were digital natives having the most analog experience of their lives, a generation known for moral fluidity being drawn to repentance under a banner of "HOLINESS UNTO THE LORD." Anyone who has come of age with a smart phone—hooked up to a little 24/7 porn store in their pocket, connected around the clock to a mini shame factory in their hand reminding them of what they are not and who they are not with—any young adult who has run the gauntlet of this cultural moment and is still walking with Jesus does so with a keen and courageous faith certainly beyond what I carried as a twenty-year-old. They lead with clarity and boldness. They know what is at stake.

The outpouring has moved me to listen to emerging adults, with their piercing insight and courageous vision, almost as I do the Old Testament prophets. The young are not rude about it but they are clear: they don't want our org charts and structures, our career ladders and programming, our metrics and trophies. Emerging adults are beginning to lead in a time when Church is seen in society as the problem, not viewed positively or even neutrally. The young live in a world that perceives Christianity as undermining the social good. So, "It's got to be real, or I'm out."

GenZ is calling us back to ourselves. This is a massive takeaway from the Asbury Outpouring. Emerging adults are beckoning the Church back to the simplicity and beauty of life in the Kingdom of

God. During the outpouring, students were unwilling to put any-one out front to lead worship who was not authentically right with Jesus. So, they closed the door on "green room" culture and invited us into "consecration room" culture. That's what was hidden behind Hughes, leading us all into the unpolished brilliance of what it's like when Jesus has the platform. It was the triumph of presence over production, of the value of integrity over the deification of talent. We had been wringing our hands and scratching our heads over how the Church would reach youth. The outpouring has helped me see how perhaps youth are coming to reach the Church.

What we have seen happening as a result of those sixteen glori-ous days and nights is the increasing empowerment and bravery of emerging leaders. They taught us to linger, be unrushed, wait on the Lord, strain a bit longer, and see what He will do. All this was nothing more than the instruction of Jesus after the ascension to return to Jerusalem and wait for the promise fulfilled. In our tightly planned services and overprogrammed lives, however, we have essen-tially forgotten how to wait, squeezing out any space where Jesus can actually enter in. Many times during the outpouring, I would hear Him whisper to me, "David, I appreciate you Western Christians with all your excellence and facilities and resources. I have done just about all I could with that. But I want you to look in Hughes and see what I can do if you just give Me the room." Our young adults led us into that.

Everywhere I look, I see young Christians ready to do the same. The outpouring taught us that if we, the middle-aged and elders, will move back and give them room, simply caring for their souls and being shade over their boldness, they will lead where Jesus is wanting to go. He wants to rescue them. Emerging adults today do not have to be known as the generation of anxiety, depression, and death. We saw them before our very eyes become young men and women of freedom and joy and life.

Provoking the Church

The outpouring is challenging us to grapple with the frustrations of youth and take on their critique. We are facing repentance over the Church we have given them and inviting them to stand on our legacy, compromised as it seems to them—that our ceiling might be their floor. This is a moment to empower the young, not only because our churches are hemorrhaging them away, but also because we need the goading of their hard questions and the blessing of their sacrificial, passionate, pioneering hearts at the vanguard of awakening.

We need a Barnabas generation before we will have an awakening generation: men and women who seek out the young like Barnabas did Saul; we will need to lend our credibility to them, journey patiently with them as they bump around in Kingdom work, and then step back as they come into their calling. Anyone today above the age of forty-five or fifty: we should do nothing except behind or beside a young leader. We are out of time for building our careers. That stuff simply does not matter anymore.

Not from any particular theological reflection or well-developed planning, our little rag-tag team stewarding the outpouring fell into the posture of nameless plurality merely from the recognition that what was happening was sacred. We dared not lay a hand or make a claim on it. So, up front in Hughes was a rotating handful of men and women who were supporting and stewarding. We never introduced ourselves. We never introduced the person coming next because it simply did not matter. Almost accidentally, we stumbled our way into a pattern that was so compelling to the young: that no one was platform-building, no one was trying to eke out a bit of personal gain on the side. That made the room feel real. Multiple unnamed speaking leaders with deeply consecrated worship leaders created one of the most humble, pure-hearted atmospheres I have ever known in my life. It became a throne room. Jesus could do anything He needed or wanted to do because He was so unusually, extraordinarily unobstructed.

This is provoking us. The outpouring was a toppling of celebrity Christianity, reminding us that while the world has big shots and stars, the Church has saints. Saints are recognized later on, usually after they have passed, for their humility and sacrifice. Celebrities work to build fame in their lifetime. Way too much of the time, American Christianity has put trust in celebrity and notoriety to draw a crowd. But church-hurt and oversold GenZ ventured to Wilmore knowing there were no marquee names to come and see. We came to understand that wherever Jesus is known to be present and working, nothing else is needed. No celebrities. Only Jesus.

The outpouring is making us take a hard look at the well-worn and failing strategies of American Christianity, calling us onto the narrow ridgeline of awakening leadership. We walk a path of avoiding the ditch of fear on one side, allowing God to be God. Young adults want all of Him in all of life and are hungry for His real presence. And we avoid the ditch of excess on the other side, moving forward collaboratively in honest, trusted, safe, empathic friendships where the Spirit can speak and transform.

The Pace of Friendship

Those friendships, we have come to understand, are not a sidebar concern in our hopes for a better day. The quality of our relationships is front and center in importance to Jesus and His work in the world. I have sometimes wished He had set up anything else as the one great necessity of His presence! Our relationships are so challenging, and the hard work of unity is so demanding. But we know it from His own words, and we saw it during the outpouring: the Kingdom of God advances at the pace of friendship. Awakening is no plug-and-play program that we can order from Amazon or pick up at the latest conference. The fullness and wholeness of God moves in the streams and currents of our love for one another, making our friendships—their humility and health—mission-critical to the work of God.

For the first few days of the outpouring, it seemed that repentance and forgiveness were almost all we could do. All over the room, people were making their way to another, tumbling over one another to make the first move of offering apologies, owning mistakes, forgiving grievances, and explaining misunderstandings. The front steps of Hughes were populated by people on their phones sending texts of reconciliation and restoration.

And inside our little stewardship circle, our relationships remained our utmost concern. Decisions of daily-increasing gravity were being made in real time, with demanding implications on many university staff and volunteers, not to mention the thousands of guests flooding into Wilmore. The stakes were too high not to be honest and direct. But time was too short for well-sequenced team processing. We had to covenant that no one would storm out of the room, no one would walk away. It was a commitment to being unoffendable, keeping short accounts, owning and apologizing instantly with the promise of deeper resolving when time would allow. But relationships had to be cared for and preserved at all costs.

Sarah has shared the story, too, in the epilogue about the depth of repentance that was confronted in our relationships spanning time across the line of race. There were important moves preceding the outpouring of community and institutional leaders who had suffered rifts and wounds in relationships decades earlier. Way before the outpouring, these men and women had traveled to Wilmore to revisit what had happened, embrace better understandings, and make amends.

Coursing through all dimensions of the outpouring from minute one were relationships that had been forged through challenge and proven sturdy, friendships that could bear the weight of forth-rightness, older stewards who could tolerate the rebuke of the young, and men and women who knew Jesus was mercifully tabernacling in the community of radical humility we had followed Him to form. When people ask, as they often have, "Is there anything we can do to have outpouring where we are? And when Jesus gives it, what can we do to steward it?" I always say, "Do whatever it takes to be sure all your relational channels are open—and stay open." We simply cannot afford to sweep our grudges under a rug and think that God doesn't see them. The outpouring taught us the joy of going first, the beautiful gift of repentance and reconciliation. We came to see the burden of unity as a labor of love, becoming the posture for prayer God seemed so pleased to answer.

The Call to Prayer

Perhaps this is the most important lesson of all from the outpour-ing. Everything that happened in Hughes Auditorium those sixteen days was the fruit of prayer. And ever since, I have never been more motivated to pray. I looked into the tear-soaked eyes of young adults experiencing *re*construction of their faith. If we could have seen that old altar rail of Hughes with spiritual eyes, we would not have seen wood. We would have only seen chains of emotional and spiritual bondage that had fallen off thousands. I beheld the joy in faces of people encountering Jesus, finding freedom from addiction and dark influences, of men and women experiencing renewal and calling and wholeness. And it convinced me that if that is what God does in response to prayer, I will carry with me forever the most compelling incentive to pray.

Over and over, as people would come into Hughes, I would greet them—from Nevada or Norway, from Argentina or Alabama.

"Wow! You've made it all the way here to Kentucky!" I would say. "Thank you for coming." And they would correct me. "Don't thank me. I *had* to come. I had to get here and put my eyes on what I have been praying for all these years!" Long before February of 2023, intercession had become a personal, spiritual stake in the ground for men and women all over the world longing for what only God can do. So, this was their Outpouring, what they had seen with spiritual eyes at altars and in closets of prayer far beyond our knowing. We said often that "the outpouring was the anti-Las Vegas. In Vegas they say, 'What happens here, stays here.' But with the outpouring, what happens here is meant for the ends of the earth!" People from all over had been praying, and this story was theirs.

I believe the great call from the outpouring is for us to fall in love with our closets again, to know the secret place as the discovery zone of what we need most in our hearts, homes, churches, and cities. Jesus Himself is the reward. Jesus alone is our identity and hope, our tenacity and courage, our motive and mission. As in every great and shaping move of God in history, we need once again to see all of ministry and all of life as an errand from the closet. Finding once more the allure and perfect satisfaction of communion with Jesus will be what opens the door for the long-expected increase of His grace in our day.

During the outpouring, every day we would hold up a phone and say, "Go ahead and take a few photos. Get a quick video. And then put your phone down. Awakening is not the same as 'going viral.' Outpouring doesn't move by looking at it on our phones, but by seeking God for it on our faces." And that fact is making more sense all the time. We are experiencing the Ezekiel 47 water levels of prayer rising as men and women everywhere, most notably in the West, are becoming more desperate for what only God can do.

When the emotionally honest expression of our prayer is proportionate to the crushing assessment of our urgent need, we begin to allow the Spirit's groanings to find utterance in us. We add our faith to these prayers of God, wrap our unity around them, and then watch Him go to work. These are days when the Spirit is wanting to reintroduce us to the Gethsemane love of travailing prayer, petitioning God as did Paul for the Galatians, like a woman in childbirth, that Christ would be formed in this generation. The outpouring drew us back to the epicenter of God's working found not in pulpits or blogs, not in books or tweets, but in closets.

The Time Is Now

A recent study by the Pinetops Foundation called *The Great Opportunity*[1] concluded that if current trends continue, over one million emerging adults at least nominally connected to the American Church today will choose to leave each year for the next three decades. That translates into nearly forty million millennials and Gen Z, currently identifying themselves as Christians, who will say that they are not by 2050. This study showed that if we could just slow the bleeding, if we could return to retention rates and evangelism patterns we saw with Generation X only two decades ago, this hemorrhaging could be reduced to a loss of twenty million.

And that twenty million difference? Holding on to those twenty million young believers would be greater than the number of all who came to faith in the First and Second Great Awakenings, the 1857 revival in New York, the Azusa Street revival, and every Billy Graham crusade *combined*. The outpouring has led us to believe that now could be our great opportunity.

We know that most people make their faith commitments by age twenty-five. The majority of millennials are now past that point, and Gen Z, the largest generation quickly becoming the most secular

1. Greatopportunity.org.

Afterword by David Thomas

generation in American history, has just now begun aging through
that milestone. The youngest Gen Z will be thirty-five by the year
2050, the age after which religious commitments generally remain
unchanged.[2] Clearly, it is no exaggeration to recognize how these next
two or three decades are make-or-break for American Christianity.

"There is a wide-open door for a great work here," Paul wrote
the Corinthians (I Cor 16:9 [NLT]), and we could say the same of our
moment now. In the outpouring, we came to see that these are not
times of spiritual hunger. More accurately, we are living in an epoch
of spiritual starvation. The waves of people pressing in during the
outpouring, traveling for days, queuing for hours, seemed akin to
what we could imagine of the throngs pressing in to be close to Jesus
for receiving His relieving, healing touch. In February 2023, it was
as though we were moving about in the pages of the New Testament.

And like Mary Peckham, this will be a story we retell for the re-
mainder of our lives. The Old Testament recounts how after Joshua's
generation "had been gathered to their fathers, another generation
grew up, who knew neither the Lord nor what he had done for Is-
rael" (Joshua 2:10). This was the state of things in post–World War II
Scotland, and it had been the same for our era until the outpouring.
Every emerging generation must come to know for themselves who
God is and how He works. And that is what He gave us in February
of 2023.

More than sixteen days and nights of His presence, Jesus gave
us a story. We saw what He can do. And we learned how it appears
He wants to be doing it. "The Lord has done great things for us, and
we are filled with joy" (Psalm 126:3 NIV)—this was the air we were
breathing in the outpouring. And it will be the testimony we will be
passing on so long as there is breath in these lungs. We will be thank-
ing God for the outpouring and asking for more.

---

2. Ibid.

His presence was too beautiful, our need for it too great, and our God is too worthy to settle for anything less.

Lexington, KY
Early Winter 2024

Acknowledgments

Asbury students of the 2022–2023 academic year, God started with you. What began in you reached around the world and will influence generations to come. You are a generation awakened. Thank you to the students who shared their testimony, read scripture, and preached during the outpouring—and do so even now around the world. Your witness continues.

Thank you, Asbury Gospel Choir, for holding the door open for the Holy Spirit on February 8 and beyond—Belle, Ben, Caleb, Charity, Donovan, Dorcus, Emma, Georges, Lena, Macie, Marie, Nathanael, Sarah.

To the Asbury University staff and faculty, you said yes thousands upon thousands of times. Your sacrificial service scaffolded a remarkable work of God. I could never begin to thank and acknowledge everyone who had a role. However, some of you I served alongside—and so a special thanks to: Ben Black, Jonny Adkins, Pam Anderson, Kevin Bellew, Joe Bruner, Barb Boyle, Kristi Boss, Taylor Collingsworth, Christine Endicott, Paul Dupree, Glenn Hamilton, Carter Hammond, Carolyn Hampton, Lisa Harper, David Hay, Laura Haugen, Brenda Hilbert, Esther Jadhav, Joe Kelly, Sam Kim, Michelle Kratzer, Abby Laub, Emily Leininger, Rob Lim, Liz Louden, Zachary Massengale, Jennifer McChord, Colin McGlothlin, Andy Miller, Don Mink, John Morley, Andy Neyman, Matt Penny, Dan Pinkston, Sherry Powers, Paul Stephens, Blake Sunny, Mark Troyer, Nathan Vick, Sheryl Voigts, and Eric Walsh. And ministry center

Acknowledgments

directors, thank you!—James Ballard, Paul and Alma Cain, Josh and Kelly Hallahan and David Schnake.

Thank you, Outpouring Core Team of 8—Madeline Black, Jeannie Banter, Kevin Brown, Zach Meerkreebs, Greg Haseloff, David Thomas, Mark Whitworth—we stood up under the outpouring of God together and we will never be the same. *Come on God, let's do it again!* #revivalbonding

Seedbed, Asbury Seminary community, Wilmore community, and many more friends, you came at just the right moment. There is no way to name everyone, but a few that I connected with during those days whom I specifically want to thank—to you I am forever grateful: thank you Jessica Avery, Mark Benjamin, Brenna Bullock, Jerry Coleman, Joanna Coppedge, Jason Duncan, Nathan Elliot, Alicia Files, Jen Haseloff, Jessica LaGrone, Luke Long, Matthew Maresco, K.O., Brandon "Shook" Shook, Bud Simon, Mark Swayze, Austin and Maddie Wofford, J.D. Walt, and Dan Wilt.

An enormous thank you to Len Wilson, Lori Wagner, and the team at Invite Resources. Thank you for your vision for this book and your encouragement along the way. Thank you, Shannon Liu, for being an early reader with excellent feedback. Thank you, Margaret Feinberg, for your incredible support.

To my husband, Clint, you are my biggest fan and encourager, always. *Thank you from the bottom of my heart.*

SCAN HERE to learn more about Invite Press, a premier publishing imprint created to invite people to a deeper faith and living relationship with Jesus Christ.